I0026662

Did You Ever Have the Teacher

Stories from People Who Survived Their Education

Nelson M. Russell

Educational
Navigating
Learning
Publishing

Williamstown, MA

Did You Ever Have the Teacher

Copyright © 2011 by Nelson M. Russell

All rights reserved.
No part of this book may be reproduced or transmitted
in any form or by any reason, electronically or mechanically,
including photography, recording, or by any information
storage system, without the express permission in writing
from the copyright owner.

Published in the United States of America,
by Navigating Learning Educational Publishing,
Williamstown, Massachusetts.

www.NavigatingLearning.com

ISBN-13   978-0-9753776-0-4
ISBN   0-9753776-0-4
CIP & LCCN data available

Printed and bound in the United States of America

First Edition

10 9 8 7 6 5 4 3 2 1

This book is dedicated
to
Stan Whitehead

He was my teacher and
mentor and guided me
through the process of
making this
book a reality.

He taught me much about
life, and passed away
just after the book
was completed.

✂～～✂

And special thanks
to
Lynn Stowe Tomb

Without her insights,
knowledge, patience
and generosity, I would
never have been able to
start this book, let alone
finish it.

Table of Contents

I – Teachers Do That   14

    Teacher's do That?   15
    Mariah   16
    Frankenstein   18
    In Harmony   20
    Good Morning BJ   22
    The Teacher Who Kicked   24
    A Third Grader   25
    Vermont French Teacher   26
    Live a Sincere and Thoughtful Life   28
    My Teacher the Janitor   30
    Aren't We All Teachers?   31

II – Empathy   32

    Favorite Teacher   33
    The Secret Garden   35
    Teachers of the Craft   36
    Or Your Worst Nightmare   39
    So Far, So Good   42
    Sister Militant   44
    Taught Us Empathy   48
    Better Under Pressure   50
    Quality of Life   52

III – Power   54

    Funny What You Can Learn if You Listen   55
    A Negotiated Settlement   56
    A Coach for Life   58
    Coach's Story   60
    Talking Hands   62
    Princess & the Pee   63
    Long-term Effects   64
    Narcissus 101   66
    Catholic Stutterer   68
    Afghan Woman   69
    Who's Being Protected?   72

IV – Boundaries   76

    Not Enough Space   77
    Don't Call Me Out   80
    Science Fair?   82
    For Better or Worse   84
    Plagiarism   86
    Favoritism   89
    Humiliation is ...   92
    Look Within   94
    Space Invaders   95

V – Expectations   96

How do We Know What We Know?   97
The Buck Stops Here   100
Banned Words   102
Ditto That   104
Class Struggle - More or Less?   105
Shakespeare Man   106
It Isn't Fair   108
Tell'em What You're Gunna Tell'em   110
Disorganized Teacher   112
A Better Match   114
I Like it When...   116
Have-a-Heart   118
Where Were You?   119

———————————

VI – Visible   120

How To Get Your Teacher Off Track   121
Class A   123
Amazing Science Teacher   124
A Separate Piece   126
Collaborate   128
A Place to Hide   130
Two Teachers   132
Stay Out of Ice Cream Shops   134
Piece of Ice   136
Letter to My Teacher   138
Against the Odds   140
Birthday Wish   141

VII – Trust   142

    Endocarditis   143
    In Teacher We Trust   144
    Pregnant at 16   148
    Shepherds and Teachers   150
    Bad Grader   152
    Under God   154
    Final Examination   156
    Children of Greenhorns   158
    My Dog Ate Them   160
    Trust and Connection   162

VIII – Connected   164

    Vernal Equinox   165
    Mrs. Rich   167
    Got Milk?   169
    The Grass is Always Greener   170
    Enthusiastic Teacher   172
    Younger Sister   174
    Twinkle of an Eye   176
    Teach Me a New Word   178
    Out of Juice   181
    Ask Yourself   182
    Music Of My Heart   183
    Epilogue   184

Reference to the Quotes   187

Introduction

"Books influence individuals; and individuals influence history ... after all, society is made up of millions of individuals".

Denise Levertov

———————

Just hearing the word "school" still seems, for many, to evoke a response from someplace deep inside. We never forget that span of time that ushered us into our adulthood, nor the teachers who brought us through it. They were there to teach, but also, in one way or other, to help form our values, our social and citizenship skills, and our sense of what is right and wrong. It is this "meta-education," the human stuff, and the teachers who influenced us that seem to linger long after what we were taught has lost its luster.

Think back to our own teachers and remember the classroom experience. Some were positive, formative events while perhaps others were burdens. What was it that happened in the second grade that might have made a child afraid of speaking out? What was it that a teacher did in science class to instill the desire to reach for new worlds? We might have had a teacher who left scars, or hopefully one who was and perhaps still is a source of inspiration.

Now though, after having been students, no matter what our work, where we do it, or whom we influence, we find ourselves in every walk of life being teachers in some way. We know the vulnerability that students feel, and as a result, share the responsibilities that come with teaching. Imagine how we could improve by listening to our collective experience, both as students and as teachers.

The book explores those experiences. It allows us to share the variety of ways in which teachers affected us, and lets us consider the impact. It brings together our stories and feelings about what teachers have done for us, both the wonderful achievements and the things that need to be done better. Perhaps teaching is a noble endeavor, but still, the things that distract us from our lofty goals might be the making of someone's educational trauma. So don't expect a "Chicken Soup" book about teaching. These stories range from the inspiring to the upsetting, each providing some insight into the impact that we have on others through our teaching, and shed some light on the things we could change.

The goal is discovery about what education was and is for us, and of what happened at school that evokes emotions and memories. Whether with joy or dread, this goal, and the stories that give insight to the answers, were the genesis of this project.

As I began to collect material for the book, I noticed an interesting response. I would barely start to explain the idea, and would soon be interrupted with… "Oh yah, Mr. Hanrahan, seventh grade. He used to…"

It resonated. It seems we are eager to share the experiences of our education, accumulated over the years. A world of insight into what education does, is revealed by these tales, and through them, we might become more compassionate and effective teachers, employers, parents, and individuals.

Nelson M. Russell

About The Book

"Every man is a quotation from all his ancestors."
                    Ralph Waldo Emerson

"Did You Ever Have the Teacher" is organized into several broad categories such as "trust" and "boundaries, etc." By considering these categories, I hope the stories can serve as a source for self-reflection on our own educational experiences and of ourselves as teachers. It is also intended as a resource for teachers, both new and experienced, to think about and discuss the issues and dilemmas faced in teaching, both pedagogical and interpersonal. The chapters and stories follow a set format. Each story will have a title and a quote. It might then start with an introductory comment and then the story. The appearance of a large capitalized letter, indicates that it is the start of someone's "teacher story." Researching the quotations was a lot of fun. See page 187 if you are interested in the person to whom the quote is attributed.

As I started to say in the introduction, when I began to collect stories they were conveyed to me by letter, email, or by someone personally sharing it with me. I also met in schools and organized meetings where people shared their stories and talked about those issues that were important to them. Whether I was in a restaurant or on an airplane, people would start telling their "teacher story." Sometimes I would take notes or record them. Other times I would reconstruct the story later on. In certain cases I combined stories which touched on the same issues but each contained thoughtful comments.

Many stories are deeply personal and moving, sharing the many wonderful ways teachers have helped shape peoples' lives. Others tell of the things that may have been much more difficult. Because of the potential for negative stories to be hurtful, I have changed the names associated with them.

Whenever a drawing appears though, the artist's name is given right next to it. Most of the drawings are done by school children from around the world. I have included their age and where they are from. Many of these images have been reprinted from the Global Children's Art Gallery (naturalchild.org/gallery), with permission from the Natural Child Project (naturalchild.org).

Nil A., age 5
Ankara, Turkey

One last thing; this book has adopted the use of the "plural/singular." for certain pronouns. When it can be avoided, instead of using "he/she" or "his/her;" "they" or "their" is used. It seems less awkward to me; perhaps it will to you too.

"The use of a third-person plural pronoun to refer to a singular pronoun was first used as early as 1300, and many writers since then prefer to use them."

The American Heritage Dictionary
(That's not to say they approve of it)

"Then the time came when the risk it took to remain tight in the bud was more painful than the risk it took to blossom."

Anais Nin

Teachers Do That?

Chapter One

*"Forgive Oh Lord my little jokes on Thee,
and I will forgive Thy great big one on me."*
                                    Robert Frost

Teachers Do That?

Recently I started a conversation
with a woman I recognized from the
local town meeting. The school budget
had been discussed and in finding something in common she asked if I were
interested in education. I told her I was
a teacher. "Oh!" she exclaimed, seem-
ing to approve. Then she followed with
a more specific question, "What do you
teach?" With a little hesitation, as not
everyone loved their high school science,
I volunteered…"I teach chemistry and
physics." At this she winced a little,
looked at me and said "Oh God, you do
that to people?"

Helen U., Age 10
Ontario, Canada

Mariah

"Far away, there in the sunshine, are my highest aspirations. I may not reach them, but I can look up and see their beauty, believe in them and try to follow where they lead."

Louisa May Alcott

After school one day a 12th grade student of mine, Mariah, came into my classroom to offer me this next story. She had heard about this book and like many it made her think of one very important teacher who had changed her life. Her teacher was a colleague of mine and at the end of the school year I shared this story with her. After reading it, she thanked me with a big smile, and tears in her eyes. Here's what Mariah wrote:

Robin N., age 12
Oklahoma, USA

"Have you ever had the kind of teacher that pushed you to do the things you were capable of? I have. Her name was Miss Seamen. Unlike any other teacher that I've had in high school, she saw that what I needed was a little push. No other teacher has done that for me and no other teacher stayed with me until I succeeded. She believed in me.

16

"I had always been discouraged by other teachers who never suggested or pushed or gave me hope. But she broke everything down and helped me see that I did have it in me to do what I put my mind to. She opened my mind and taught me new skills. These were skills that I would use in the workplace, and even in the community, to help me help others.

"I can remember days when I was not in the mood to do anything. She had a way to change that. Even when I was hard on her, she would never let it get to her. She just kept smiling and encouraging me.

"One skill I thank her so much for is sign language. She taught me about deaf culture and how to go about working with the deaf. She taught me how to sign and how to read signs. I feel as if she is not there just as a teacher but also as a friend.

I know that if I ever needed help in school or advice in my personal life that she would be there with a smile on her face and a helping hand. So, I guess what I'm trying to say is Thank You. If it were not for you pushing me, I don't know where I would be right now, or what I would want to do in life."

Mariah K.

Frankenstein...

"Did you ever have the teacher who gave you the chills? I did. The whole class would shake when she was mad. I tell you I will never forget her."

When I invited people to share their teacher stories, this was the very first response that I received. Whatever it is that teachers do, good or bad, people never seem to forget them. When you ask someone to reminisce about a teacher, there is no hesitation. They start telling their story, with all the details. I remember my fourth grade teacher, Miss O'Hara, both fondly and with dread. She used to hit me on the head with her hand that had that big ring on it. It hurt, but at least she wasn't Frankenstein.

"She was just one of those people who had a loud voice, very strong personality, and just had a mean face. You knew you were busted with just a look, no words. In our school we had no other choice for a teacher - there was only one teacher for every grade. There was no escape! So picture this: I'm in the sixth grade, the building was so old you'd think we lived in the country but this was in the Bay Area.

"Anyways, this was at a time when there were elementary schools in the neighborhood, and we all knew that we would get this teacher sooner or later. From the first day it was known that there would be no horseplay and no fun. God forbid we even looked at the clock to see when our torment was over, that would add one minute to her 'After School Program' (which you might know as detention) for the whole class.

"We were not allowed to speak unless spoken to. We learned to drink enough water, use the rest room, and sharpen pencils during recess. If we made that fatal mistake of doing any of the above during class time, that would add more time to the 'After School Program.'

"When my sister and I remember her, we always remember she owned an orange Corvette, which at the time was something out of Hollywood. Our neighborhood was mostly kids whose parents worked in the cannery and rode in old station wagons or walked. She was a tall woman, pale white, pitch-black hair, red, red lipstick. She wore white pants and black polka dot underwear. We often wondered if she even knew. 'Hello, we can see through the pants!' I think she knew. She was not a dumb woman. But if you stuck two bolts on her neck she would look just like Frankenstein! Really she did.

"What did I learn from her, in terms of knowledge? Nothing, I say. I do not even know how we all passed. I was an extremely shy, nervous kid, and her way of teaching did nothing for me. It made me scared to ask for help. But I did learn what teachers *should* do. That is why when my daughter was younger, I made sure to check out what kind of teacher she had, what teaching methods were used, and what the discipline was like. You get your legitimacy from the people you teach. So I guess that is what she taught me: be very aware of people calling themselves teachers."

Tracy R.

Taylor E., age 4
Oregon, USA

In Harmony

"What you see and hear depends a great deal on where you are standing; it also depends on what sort of person you are."

C. S. Lewis

It seems hard sometimes to tell what makes a great teacher or even a good one. This story is among several that show us how a sense of perspective can sometimes change your opinion. Teachers who you thought were great because they didn't push you and were so easy, can become the teachers who you later resent for having let you down. Those teachers whom you "hated" for their high expectations, for how they made you work, or how they pushed you, may be the ones you come to appreciate the most later on.

Elsa I., Age 9
Ontario, Canada

"When I was in junior high school - I guess it's called 'middle school' now - I was made to take music. I didn't do it by choice. My voice wasn't that good and I really didn't like music. But I had to go to it every day. Back then I didn't like my teacher. What appeared to me then as her being fed up with us, I see now as her really wanting something better for us and to open up the whole world of music to us.

"Our resistance was sometimes difficult for her. I remember how upset she would get when a few of the boys in the class would talk and joke among themselves. They weren't mean spirited, not really disrespectful; they just liked to laugh and tell jokes and had no interest in music. Kind of like me but I behaved. She would clang down on the piano keyboard. Sometimes she'd get so upset she'd almost cry.

"I didn't appreciate that teacher then but now I do. I'm so thankful to have had Mrs. Longman as a music teacher. She was so dedicated. She truly cared about her students and had a passion for music. If it weren't for her I would live in a world of limited musical appreciation. Instead I have been given the capacity to appreciate a world of music, its spectrum and variety.

"She taught us to sing a wide range of songs, from show tunes to obscure tunes, to popular music. We sang the 'Hallelujah Chorus" from Handel's *Messiah*, tunes from *The Sound of Music*, you name it. We learned of music from Asia, Africa, and South America, all over. She brought the world of music to us. It seemed that then we didn't really care, but now I do.

"She taught us music theory. She would bring in recordings of music for us to listen to and to share what we thought. She had us put on a production of *South Pacific* (in appropriate costumes), and we sang at school assemblies and at other places in the community, like retirement homes. Even though we didn't really understand it then, it meant a great deal to us and gave us a sense of giving. She wanted so much for us to learn about music. I did, and my life is richer for it."

Kelsie L.

Good Morning, BJ

*"Good teachers are costly but bad teachers
end up costing a whole lot more"*

Bob Talbert

The next four stories explore how some teachers abuse
authority, betray trust, or demonstrate that they lack the empathy
to understand their students. When students enter a classroom,
all they have is their trust in their teacher. It can be a very lonely
experience when the teacher violates that trust, crosses that
boundary, and mistreats one student while co-opting the other
students to join in. In this case he becomes a bully, an abuser.
Aren't teachers supposed to be significant role models for
students? Think of that special teacher who influenced how you
treat others. One can only imagine what signal the behavior in
this story sent, and can only guess at the teacher's motivation.

"My friend John, who is now a successful
business owner in London and whose accountant
has given him a strict budget of spending no
more than $30,000 a year for his vacations (poor
guy) tells a story of growing up in Kansas City,
where his health-class teacher used to make fun
of him in class, in front of the other kids.

"This teacher used to come in and say, 'Class,
do you want to say good morning to BJ today?'
(Now John's name or initials weren't BJ – one
can only assume that the teacher was ridiculing
him because he was scrawny and effeminate.

"The class would chant, 'Good morning, BJ!'
And then this lovely teacher would bend over
and pick John up by the ankles, lifting him into
the air and upside down, shaking him so that

things in his pockets would fall out. And how the other children would laugh.

"This was freshman year of high school. Some days, in the middle of class, the teacher would say, 'Hey kids, should we say good morning to BJ again?' You get the idea.

"I can't say how the experience changed him directly. It made his life during a sensitive period very difficult and painful. But I will say that now he's very conscious, as a rich guy, never to mistreat his driver or his mailman, or show any disrespect to the people around him. For the most part, he was able to move beyond this experience; that's just the Midwesterner in him. None the less it had an impact.

"John is 39 now, and chooses not to go back to his high school. When he tells this story, he shakes his head in bewilderment: 'How could an adult, especially a teacher, ever be so cruel to a child?' This teacher somehow thought he was funny, and never questioned the correctness – after all, he got the response he wanted from the other students."

Lily W.

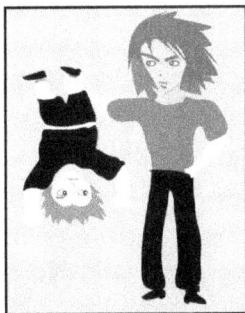

Simegen facsimile

The Teacher Who Kicked...

"Remember, nobody will ever get ahead of you as long as they are still kicking you."

Walter Winchell

There are those teachers who think their abusive behavior somehow serves the greater good of teaching. Then there are those teachers, as in the last story, who lack judgment and have lost the insight into why they teach or how they treat their students. These teachers may not know why they act the way they do, but students never forget what happened. Some of the stories describe really inappropriate behavior. What drives teachers' abusive behavior and how do they justify it? There are those teachers who find themselves doing battle with their students, consumed with control, or who are driven by their own demons. This story is told by someone who remembers clearly, and is among many about control over going to the bathroom.

"When I was in the fourth grade, we had a teacher who should have been considered a child abuser. She was always angry. As a regular practice, she made disruptive little boys sit under her desk while she finished the class period. If they still misbehaved, she kicked them with her pointed high heels. She never did this to the girls.

"It wasn't unusual that, after making the boys go under her desk, she would punish us all. On one occasion, when she was particularly upset with several children, she didn't let anyone leave the classroom for three hours. It happened to be a rainy day, so no one would have noticed that we weren't outside at recess. When I say we couldn't leave the classroom; I mean not at all. Not even to use the rest rooms. You can imagine…"

Lorriane M.

24

A Third Grader

*"Every time I paint a portrait
I lose a friend."*
John Singer Sargent

"As a high school student I really wanted to learn how to paint. I was painting a picture in art class. The teacher looked at it and said:
'That looks like it was done by a third-grader.'
I never painted another picture..."

Jaye D.

Erling M., age 6
Kolbotn, Norway

25

Vermont French Teacher

*For every reaction there is an
equal and opposite action.*

Unknown

When lack of respect and class-mismanage-
ment lead to the teacher's slippery slope…

———————

"My high school in northern Vermont had
many French students visiting as part of an
exchange program from Quebec, Canada.
Although the exchange students spoke French,
being from a French-speaking province, they
were required to join in with our French class.
The French teacher for our school was an
American who had learned to speak French in
France. She had lived in Paris and had studied
at the Sorbonne. She spoke French beautifully,
as she was always sure to let us know. We were
a little embarrassed, but she was not very
tolerant of the Canadians' accent. Just as with
the English and Americans, a person speaking
French Canadian can sound very different from
a Parisian who is speaking the same language.
To us it all seemed like fun. We didn't care, but
she did.

"Teaching English-speaking students French
is one thing because the language is entirely new
to them, but it is very different to attempt to teach
French to students from Quebec. The Canadians
already spoke the language; they just spoke it a
little differently than the teacher. The teacher
was having a difficult time accepting this
difference and was lashing out at the students.

'You are not speaking proper French'; she would say. 'You are mispronouncing everything; it is too guttural.' Being in class was awful. You could see she was offending the Canadian students. The students and teacher began to view each other as enemies.

"The visiting students complained to their host families. 'She was telling us that our French was not good enough, that it was not as good as hers,' said one of the students.

"The teacher felt frustrated and the students felt angry. The class had begun to lose respect for her. Why shouldn't they have? She was not respecting them or giving them any support for who they were or for their culture. Arguments between the teacher and our students began, and each class became more like a place to do battle than a place to learn.

"One day the teacher erupted in anger at her students, telling them that they were disrespectful and unwilling to learn how to speak French properly. 'You cannot learn with this attitude,' she said, 'your attitude is half of the problem.'

"One of the visiting students immediately quipped back, 'Oui, et vous êtes l'autre moitie' ('ya, and you're the other half')."

Jonathan R.

Lacey P., age 9
Virginia, USA

Live A Sincere And Thoughtful Life...

'Treat a man as he is, he will remain so. Treat a man the way he may be and ought to be, and he will become as he can be and should be."

Goethe

Oh, if we all could be Mr. Pierini...

"This is about my fifth grade teacher at my elementary high school in California. Mr. Pierini changed my life and my love of learning. I was a very shy little girl. On the first day of class, I brought my glasses, and held them in my hands, embarrassed to put them on, since only 'nerds' wore glasses. He must have seen me because Mr. Pierini, after introducing himself, looked around the room, and announced, 'I wear glasses, so anyone else in the class who wears them should put them on now. If you can't see, you can't learn.' I snuck a look around the room, and then put them on. He looked right at me (he was very good at making direct eye contact), and said, 'Now, that's better,' and got on with the lesson.

"That year, in Mr. Pierini's class, I did the best I've ever done in math. When we did really well he encouraged us with ice cream sundaes, which he bought out of his own pocket. The biggest treat of all was being with him after class; he was so attentive. He spent a lot of extra time with us kids.

"That was also the year I began to write. During class, Mr. Pierini read poems and stories to us. I started to think poetically, and even brought in a long poem about space creatures, which we worked on together during recess or breaks. I loved that poem and still remember verses of it.

"I felt so special, and I found a love of writing and of poetry within myself. This love continued. Later on in high school I won two poetry awards in the New York City school district where I later went to school, and then pursued writing and literature in college. Writing still remains important to me although I went into psychology as a profession.

"You could say Mr. Pierini also had an influence on me in making that decision. Every day, he brought in questionnaires, fill-in the blank quizzes and such, from books he had found on personal development for kids. His idea was to encourage us to think about who we were as human beings. Not just ask what color we liked, or what was our favorite animal, but to question what we might do in a particular stressful situation. We explored what the favorite parts of ourselves were, or who we were closest to in our families, and why. He encouraged us to think about who we were as people. Each day he allotted some time in class for us to think about and write answers to these questions. He would come around to each one of us and talk about our answers. We could also do these exercises as additional homework. He made it clear that 'who we were' was as important as 'what we did,' and to live a sincere and thoughtful life. He was a good example of that.

"A few weeks before the end of school (which I was dreading since I didn't want to have a different teacher the following year), he told us that he wanted to measure our fingers for a math project. On the last day of class, he came around to each of us and gave us sterling silver rings which he had handmade. Each one fit perfectly, and it's sentimental to say, but his teaching style was a perfect fit – individualized, attentive, and loving. I loved this teacher, and his impact on me will never stop.

"Incidentally, I did call him, three years ago, and thanked him for his wonderful influence in my life."

Heather S.

My Teacher the Janitor

"That's a horse of a different color!"
Guardian of Emerald City Gates

"Math was always very difficult for my friends and me. One day just outside the boiler room where the lockers were, we were talking about how hard it was to learn from our math teacher. Out of nowhere the janitor, Mr. Scipione, interrupted us. He had been listening to what we were saying and started to ask us what our problems were with math. With each problem he would tell us a little story about how the math worked. It made so much sense and seemed like the real world. When he gave us practice problems we were able to solve them.

"Later he offered to help us on a regular basis, but no one was to know because he wasn't a 'real teacher.' Every week on Wednesdays after school, we would meet with him for half an hour or 45 minutes and we would show him what we were working on. He would tell us little stories and show us techniques that made solving them easy. He explained it in a way that was not scary and didn't make us feel stupid. He always told us, 'Don't worry, no matter what you've been shown, or how you solve it, if you get the right answer, the math ultimately is the same – it's just a different sequence or a different setup.' That made us not quite as afraid when solving problems back in class. That was the ninth grade. My grade went from D to A level work, and I got a B for the year.

"It seems to me that Mr. Scipione was a 'real teacher.' He did this for us out of the goodness of his heart. He didn't trip-off on whatever, like regular teachers do. He had no power trip or control issues. He was a real teacher."

Jeremy L.

Aren't We All Teachers?

"The teacher who is indeed wise does not bid
you to enter the house of his wisdom but rather
leads you to the threshold of your mind."

Kahlil Gibran

"I remember – not when I was a very small child, but when I was more grown up – we would needle [my grandfather] by claiming not to believe in God and so on. You'd say, in your 10- or 11-year-old self, 'I don't believe in God, Grandad'. And he'd say, 'Oh really? Come and sit down here and tell me all about it.' And so you'd sit down next to him and he would very seriously listen and probe as you offered your 11 year-old reasons for not believing. And then, instead of contradicting you, he'd say, 'Yes, well, that's a lot to think about, I think you've given me a lot to think about, I'll have to think about it.'

"And then, a couple of days later, he'd come back and he'd say, 'I just did have a couple of thoughts about what you were saying, and let me just talk to you about them.' And he'd then offer you, in a very gentle way, his rebuttals to your childish ideas. And when you'd say, 'No, no, Grandad, that's just complete nonsense, it's completely wrong,' and you would explain why, he'd say, 'Yes, well, you're probably right, but I just think we should go on talking about it'."

An excerpt from
an Interview with
Salmon Rushdie
by Peter Kadzis
May 10, 1999

Clair J., Age 7
Paris, France

Did You
Ever Have
the
Teacher

Empathy

Chapter Two

"Education is the transmission of civilization."
Will Durant

Favorite Teacher

At the Pt. Reyes Station Memorial Day parade, I had stopped to get a hot dog from the local sandwich vendor on the side of the street. While I was waiting for my hot dog, I heard the gal behind the counter exclaim to her fellow worker; "Oh my gosh, did you see that? That was my favorite teacher!" I couldn't help but wonder what makes a "favorite" teacher.

As she was handing me my hot dog, I asked, "Tell me, what was so special about your teacher?"

Surprised a little, she repeated, "Well, she was my favorite teacher!"

Trying to share her enthusiasm, I followed-up: "What was it that actually made her your favorite teacher?"

She paused, and added, as if it were an explanation: "Well, I went to the continuation high school."

I found that interesting, having taught at one. The continuation high school is the school of last resort and can be a difficult place to teach. These students are no longer welcomed in the regular high school and this is the only remaining school for them. California schools must provide a continuation school as an alternative to expulsion or dropping out.

"But can you tell me what it was about her that made her your favorite teacher?"

"She was the dance teacher." She was getting closer.

Funny how easy it is somehow to put your finger on what you didn't like about a teacher, and have plenty to say, but then have much more difficulty articulating what made a good teacher so important to you. I asked again "What was it that she did as your teacher, that made you so happy to see her?"

She put her hands on the counter, and smiled. "It was the student-teacher thing, the people thing." And then she went on to explain: "She treated us like we were people, respected us. She encouraged me. At school she understood us, she let us feel good about ourselves. I liked being in her class."

Among the many gifts that empathy gives, is the feeling of being understood. Whatever it was that this teacher did, it clearly made a difference for this girl.

Elsa I., age 10
Connecticut, USA

The Secret Garden

"Imagination grows by exercise, and contrary to common belief, is more powerful in the mature than in the young."

W. Somerset Maugham

"Yes! – Mrs. Wilson. I was a chatterbox and in general, I suppose, a pain in the neck. In retrospect I probably had ADHD. She was my third grade teacher. I was a little difficult and she had to discipline me quite often. It was hard for her, and I didn't like it. She wanted us to get work done and I really had a hard time focusing. I guess you would say I didn't get along with her at first, but she changed that.

"She was a funny lady, kind of small, a little over-weight and she spoke with a lisp. This you would think would have caused kids to make fun of her, but not Mrs. Wilson. She seemed to command a certain respect, even from us 'trouble makers.' In the second half of the year she started a new activity. Every day after lunch she would gather us all around and she would read to us. I remember such wonderful stories as *The Secret Garden* and *The Twelve Dancing Princesses*. She would read with such animation and connectedness that I would create a world of images in my head. Sometimes she would stop and ask us to share our images. It was fun to hear how different people put the stories together differently. It helped me be more sensitive about how others think and feel. It changed me. After that she became very important to me and became my closest teacher. She helped open up a whole new world for me. It helped me calm down and it helped me live a richer life. I can't imagine a greater gift than the freedom she gave me."

Katherine D.

Teachers of the Craft

"Reality is just an illusion, albeit a very persistent one."
Albert Einstein

One hopes that teachers wish to foster the human spirit and enrich the lives of their students. Whether studying physics or learning to be a clown, one needs a skilled teacher. What are the characteristics that teachers need to have? Even if you were to study witchcraft, you would want a teacher who can have a positive impact, and have empathy for you as a learner and a person. What is a good teacher? Here is an edited excerpt of two stories from the *Witches Voice*[*]and what they consider to be the qualities necessary for a good teacher, and what to avoid, if you want to learn the "craft." There are many ways to "pass along the knowledge," but the fundamentals of a good teacher remain, no matter the subject. Here are their qualities ...

Lee E., age 6
Beer Sheve, Israel

"**G**ood teachers:

"Have a sense of humor – Learning is filled with mistakes. Good teachers will help you laugh at them and will not hold you up to ridicule.

"Have respect for all living things - One should care about the lives and welfare of animals and people and the environment, as abuse of any living thing is a no-no.

"Have a healthy self image - Teachers who realize that they can learn from a novice, just as the novice learns from them, are probably comfortable in what they know yet open to new ideas and concepts.

"Are kind and compassionate – You still have to work hard, but your honest efforts will be met with encouragement and gentle guidance. A good teacher will respect your sincere attempts, knowing that experience is necessary to gain knowledge.

"Tell the truth and are direct – A good teacher will not be afraid to confront you when you are heading in a wrong direction and never manipulate you for unspoken ends. They are always truthful and want you to be too. They 'walk their talk' and do not have a separate code of conduct for themselves and others.

"Are able to teach by example - Good teachers often share stories of their successes and failures and do so with humility, using themselves to offer practical examples and applications. They are not mysterious so much as they demonstrate the mysteries in simple ways to help you understand them.

"Have a global point of view - Local gurus may only be interested in making a name or creating a following for themselves. Good teachers will encourage students to reach out and embrace the local area and the whole world.

"Are inclusive rather than exclusive in attitude - Anyone who promotes 'us vs. them' is dangerously close to becoming a cult leader. A teacher who finds an enemy around every corner should be avoided. Good teachers create a sense of empathy and inclusion for all.

"Allow for mistakes and admit that they are not perfect. 'We are all in this together' is a good statement to hear from a teacher who you are considering working with.

"Are flexible, yet honor commitments – Good teachers know to keep a balance between a rigid set of rules, which can stifle learning, and too random a program which interferes with discipline and growth.

"Encourage you to do your own research and ask questions - A good teacher wants you to discover and explore new ideas. You should be able to respectfully disagree with a teacher without being censored or reprimanded. They may guide you to reach understanding.

"Give credit where credit is due - A teacher who uses references or techniques from others, should clearly state their sources. To use other people's work without credit is theft, plain and simple.

"Listen more than talk - A good teacher is genuinely interested in your thoughts, feelings and opinions. Feedback is one way that a teacher can tell how you are absorbing and integrating the materials and lessons. Someone who talks all the time about their experiences is more interested in impressing you with their personal knowledge than helping you to acquire knowledge of your own.

"Want you to mature and move on - Good teachers want their students to surpass them. That is the greatest compliment that a teacher can receive. Just as good parents want to send mature and well balanced children into the world, so do good teachers want their 'children' to grow and excel."

Or Your Worst Nightmare

"Vision without action is a daydream.
Action without vision is a nightmare."
Japanese Proverb

"On the other hand, you should avoid a teacher who...

"Possesses a superior attitude... If a teacher tells you that they are the sole holder of secret knowledge disclosed only to a chosen few, you really don't want to know what it is...really.

"Excludes members of any race or culture... Bigotry of any kind has no place in learning circles.

"Is attacking or violent... Obviously.

"Is too insensitive... Someone who either sees slights and attacks where there are none may not be in touch with reality. Best to leave them to their own little fantasy world.

Helen U., age 10
Ontario, Canada

"Is ingratiating... When a teacher shares intimate details of their personal life with you, they may be looking to win you over. This is a real danger sign that is often overlooked. By baring their soul, they encourage you to do the same in return. This instant intimacy can leave you vulnerable to manipulation and abuse. Go slowly when meeting someone new.

"Is controlling – No teacher should expect you to abandon your family and friends. Isolation from the rest of society is a classic cult activity. You should not be expected to do things that are uncomfortable or inappropriate. If you feel like you are being taken advantage of, you probably are.

"Fails to show up for class, or is always late – This is a classic indication that they no longer care.

"Belittles you or uses you as an example – You deserve to be treated with respect. No teacher has the right to strip you of your self-esteem. Don't work with a teacher who is a bully or with one who has class 'pets.' This type of teacher may be setting you up for something that you may not want to become involved in.

"Does not have the respect of their peers and past students – What do other teachers think of them, and what has become of past students? It pays to check. Talk to anyone you can find who has trained with this teacher in the past. You should be able to get a class schedule and class outline before you sign up. Look it over carefully and ask questions. It's not worth it if the information seems to be no more than what you can get on your own from books or by talking with others.

"The teacher, and perhaps the assistants, expect you to be obedient – Some groups do have a system of elders who deserve respect. However, you are not obligated to accept anyone simply based on their rank within a group. If the teacher has an entourage that follows them everywhere and seems to cater to this teacher's every whim, watch carefully. You may end up being the next groupie.

"Is overly idealistic and impractical – Avoid a teacher who has marvelous plans for the world, especially if they tell you that you will be a part of this grand scheme. It is made even worse if they are unable to balance their checkbook, hold onto jobs. You may end up supporting this person in ways that are outside of what is appropriate. Our path is one of personal responsibility and teachers should be able to manifest this in their own lives. If they can't, they shouldn't try to teach.

"Lacks Empathy – If the teacher genuinely does not feel the goals and the struggles of the student, they probably are not going to be able to help you get there."

---

* These two stories, "Teachers of The Craft" and "Or Your Worst Nightmare," were first presented in *The Witches Voice* by Wren Walker. It gives a very clear outline of what is important to look for when pursuing a "teacher of the craft" and, so it seems, a teacher of anything.

So Far, So good

"Individual commitment to a group effort -- that is what makes a team work, a company work, a society work, a civilization work."

Vince Lombardi

The next two stories are about teachers who lacked any apparent empathy for their students. Mrs. Annan, in this story, was able to open gates. Sister Millicent, in the following story, managed to close them. In both cases the teachers were disliked, but for Mrs. Annan it was better to be hard and disliked, and accomplish a lot. What Sister Millicent accomplished wasn't necessarily educational. In either case, somewhere in our learning-at-the-moment should lie the tools to be successful in life. Mrs. Annan seemed to be able to provide those tools, and access to the future, without an obvious empathy for the student. Sister Millicent may have helped develop tools for the future but they weren't quite the same.

"As a 16-year old high school student, I was terrified to learn that Mrs. Annan would be my honors English-Rhetoric teacher. I was a partial honors student and English was my best subject, so I was not looking forward to the teacher with the worst reputation in the school as far as grading was concerned. Well, she was every bit as bad as they had warned. She acted as if we were all pretty stupid and getting more than a C on any exam or paper was a miracle.

"If you had one single dangling participle, you would receive a skull and crossbones at the top of your paper, drawn by hand of course by Mrs. Annan (basically you earned a zero on the paper). She was strict, she was abrupt, and she looked like she should have been teaching in a 'bad-girls' boarding school.

"Once, in my two years with her, I got an A- on a fiction essay. It was like a miracle had occurred. I don't think there was a person in a 10-mile radius that didn't know about my grade. Anyway, as you might have guessed where I am going, Mrs. Annan turned out to be the best teacher I ever had. We were never 'close' and I never received the grades I thought I deserved, but she taught me and my classmates more about the English language, and how to think, than any teacher I've ever had, including those I had in college. She wasn't warm and fuzzy and she wasn't easy. She had no intention of being a friend, but she genuinely cared about our success. She set the bar high and pushed us to get there.

"As a result, she made college a breeze for me. Two of my classmates (that I know of) went on to become professional journalists and one of them mentioned Mrs. Annan (with thanks) in her column a while back.

"I use writing regularly in my profession, so I think of Mrs. Annan often. She passed away not too long ago and almost all of her past students donated to a charitable organization they were setting up in her name.

"Mrs. Annan really taught us English and not one person who I've talked to since that time (who had her as a teacher) has ever forgotten about her and they all speak of her with a kind of love and tenderness. Frankly, there have been few like her."

Nadine F.

Miranda S. age 7
Idaho, USA

Sister "Militant"

It is one thing to show someone they are in error,
and another to put them in possession of the truth.

John Locke

Empathy is a special capacity that is both innate and can be developed. When a teacher helps a student feel understood it goes a long way to eliminating fear of the learning process. As with Mrs. Annan, teachers without an obvious empathy can still be successful if they are careful to be very fair to each student and give equal access all. If they fail at empathy and fail at access, then what are they doing? For a child, the early classroom is a big part of their world. It becomes a microcosm that helps to form the world view they might have as adults. Unlike in Mrs. Annan's world, in Sister Millicent's there was no empathy or access.

"The letter came from St. Theresa, stating that my kindergarten teacher would be Sister Millicent. I was given this information as if it were good news but it wasn't. She was about my mother's age and never let go of the heavy cross at the end of the rosary she always carried. Her cropped dark hair, slightly grey, peeked from under the blue habit. Her rarely expressed smile always seemed so fake.

"In a corner of the kindergarten was an old beat up piano with a coat of orange paint. On it, Sister Millicent would chord out the two songs she knew: 'My Country 'Tis of Thee' (always after pledging allegiance), and 'Jesus Loves Me' (which was ironic, considering how much she invoked the 'Jesus figure' as a threat to keep us in line).

"Initially, I had no particular feelings toward Sister Millicent. What did I know? It was clear she was not a warm person, nor particularly creative. She would often look at children and inform them, trying to sound sad, that they weren't making any effort. If that didn't work, she would slap their hands and tell them Jesus was watching them. The big crucifix at the front of the room, with a baleful looking Jesus glaring down at us, certainly made her point. Using too much paste, breaking or losing crayons, or not being able to zip your own coat, were all things that would incur the wrath of our ever-vigilant Jesus, according to her.

"Some kindergartners had a hard time saying Sister Millicent's name and pronounced it 'Sister Militant.' That name certainly suited her better and it stuck. Although she was cold and mean, it took a while to see how deep her mean streak was.

"One day in late October Sister Martha appeared in the doorway with a small girl. She had straight short blonde hair and blue eyes. 'Sister Millicent, this is Shari.'

'What is her full name?' barked Sister Millicent sourly, looking her up and down with distaste. Behind Shari was a thin woman with unkempt hair, in shabby clothes, who looked tired. She was obviously the child's mother.

'Shari Lynn' the woman offered meekly.

"To start Shari off on the right track of mistreatment, Sister Millicent immediately and unceremoniously relegated her to the one empty table in the back of the room, as though she were a leper. 'You can sit over there,' she gestured dismissively. That was her welcome to our classroom.

"Looking back now, I wince with hatred for Sister Militant. I did not know of the world's oldest profession, or Shari's mother's affiliation with it, or why Shari would be affected by it. At age five, I could only feel uncomfortable for Shari. Still, she was exuberant, had an innocent smile, a sweet laugh and an endearing presence. In Sister Millicent's class though, she was the scapegoat. She occupied the table alone unless some other hapless student was punished; 'Go sit with Shari.'

"At one point she yelled, 'Basil, look at this terrible coloring. You're just not trying.' Slap, slap, 'Just remember: Jesus is watching you.' 'Children who don't try, make him very angry.' 'Basil! You're not even paying attention. I've had it up to here with your daydreaming.

Take your work and go sit with Shari!' Sister Millicent forgot to move me from the leper table back into the 'general population'. That was just fine with me. However, the extent of her spite had not yet come.

"Whenever birthdays occurred, that child's mother would bring cupcakes to the class to celebrate it, making sure there was enough for everyone. Usually there was enough extra for Sister Millicent and a few other choice members of the staff. Fiona's mother hadn't quite planned right. We had twenty-one children in our kindergarten. She made a mistake and brought only twenty cupcakes. Fiona's embarrassed mother was prepared to delay the 'party' and go to the bakery for more cupcakes. However, Sister Militant didn't miss a beat, 'Shari has been bad this week. She doesn't need a cupcake.' I'll never forget her monochromatic voice, the smugness of her gaze as she invoked her bitterness. Shari bit her lip. I had never seen her cry, but this was the closest.

"Fiona Farrel's mother, mouth opened, in speechless shock, tried to figure out how to tactfully overrule a nun. 'Oh no, I couldn't do that…I'll go out for more. I'll be right back…' Fiona's mother's voice trailed off and was interrupted.

"'Mrs. Farrel, school is almost over. This is when you said you'd be here. This time could be spent on other things.' After much resistance, Sister Millicent prevailed. The die had been cast. Fiona's mother had been placed in a very awkward position and everyone realized that Sister Militant had gone too far.

The cupcakes were distributed to all the children, all except Shari. Shari looked Sister Militant in the eye as she walked past her with the cupcake tray. Sister Millicent would not look back. Shari clenched her teeth together as she fought back tears. I could feel what Shari was feeling. Happy Birthday was sung, Sister Militant's robotic voice drowning out everybody else in a gloating song of vicious triumph. My conscience pricked me as I looked at Shari and wondered how I was going to be able to eat this cupcake. For the last few weeks now we were tablemates and had become friends, having incurred Sister Militant's wrath together. I surreptitiously looked around to make sure that Sister Millicent was not watching.

"I broke my cupcake in half and passed it across the table to Shari. Then Joey, half a cupcake in hand, solemnly walked over to Shari and placed it in front of her. 'Joseph, get back in your seat!' Louise got up and did the same. So did Geoffrey. And Mary. And Karen. And William. 'Children! Sit down right now!' But nobody was listening to Sister Militant.

"Soon, Shari sat bewildered before a total of ten cupcakes in pieces, like a queen before a feast. Mrs. Farrel started to cry and turned around so we wouldn't see it. Sister Militant glowered, having lost at her own game. Mrs. Farrel, by some odd method of division made sure each child got an equal piece of cupcake, including, and especially, Shari. With satisfaction, I watched Sister Millicent squirm uncomfortably. It was the justice of twenty-one five year olds, with Sister Millicent finally in possession of the truth.

Basil S.

Taught Us Empathy

"I think it's easy to mistake understanding for empathy – we want empathy so badly."
Thomas A. Harris

Being able to express empathy helps an individual to feel fulfilled and enriched in a diverse society. It should be one of our goals to teach our students ways to experience empathy, and to have empathy for others. This capacity is not necessarily developed at home. We have an opportunity though to help develop it by incorporating these experiences into our curriculum and into the culture of school or the workplace. If students can understand others' lives, they can learn to make positive, compassionate change.

———————

"I'd like to share a story about some of the teachers I had when growing up. I'm 24 now and in grad school; but I can remember my teachers clear-as-day because my experiences were so positive.

"I went to a school called Cunningham Elementary, since renamed Highline Community Elementary School. It is part of the Cherry Creek School District. I remember specifically Mrs. Coleburn, Ms. Velasquez, and Mr. Steele, and many others that weren't my teachers.

"I respect them for the innovative ways in teaching that they had. The school was ahead of its time. The teachers took us on many trips and we were taught about people and the world. We were taught about empathy, hands-on. We had projects from which we learned to 'feel.'

"These projects were like going for a day or two pretending to live the life of someone who was blind, or handicapped (in a wheelchair) to see what it felt like. I'll never forget that experience; it is still within me every day. I remember how caring and concerned the teachers were and how encouraging, and how it felt to be cared for and to care for others.

"Their philosophy was, 'every child should be given a chance for success' and that they did, and it made a big difference for me. I have a child now who is in Kindergarten and the teachers seem overworked and not able to care as much; nothing like the schools I attended.

"I wish children could be raised by a good community and feel accounted for. Unfortunately it seems we treat children like they are a problem instead of our future. I hope we can find our way back to the kind of teaching that really helps a person be able to learn, and to have empathy."

Belinda W.

Wetzel Elementary School
School-homepage.jpg

Better Under Pressure

"I was determined to know beans."
Henry David Thoreau

Many people look back on their education and evaluate it differently than when they were in the process. Rarely do they look back and wish it had been easier, or wish they had been allowed to get away without learning. Mostly there is a wish to have been better educated, better prepared, pushed harder and to have gotten further. People complain about their teachers for two main reasons: they were mistreated or they were poorly educated.

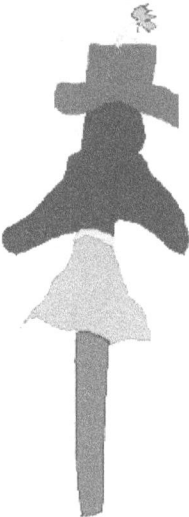

Julia M., age 9
Bremen, Germany

"The worse thing that happened to me was not being encouraged to study more. I was reasonably intelligent and could coast through the academic requirements in most of my courses without too much difficulty. Part of this was because of the school. I went to a small high school in a poor community. Like lots of small high schools, this one had an academic section and a vocational section. All the students within a program were assumed to be at the same level. So the students in the academic program were all at 'one level.' Thus, the teachers had to 'dumb down' (I hate that phrase) the academic classes to reach all the students. I rarely had much homework and nothing to push my mind.. Fortunately, I liked to read and was able to gain some extra knowledge that way.

"Having done well in my school, I received a full tuition scholarship to the University of Pennsylvania and decided (don't ask me why) to major in chemical engineering. It was really difficult and I couldn't handle the work. I hadn't been prepared by my high school. I ended up flunking a dual course of mathematics. It was because the others were very well prepared students from large high schools. Those students had already taken the math course in high school. It was all review to them, I had to start from the beginning. Not having been prepared by my education for college, and not having been pushed, resulted in a real impact on the course of my life.

"I ended up dropping out and worked in the basement stockroom of a department store. My supervisor was a woman who had been there for a long time. When I told her I was thinking about not returning to college, she lambasted me. She told me that I had an opportunity to get out of the working class and into something better. She pushed me to work hard at my job and to get myself back into school. She really seemed to understand me, and apparently much more.

"As a result, I went back to U of PA, changed my major to business and eventually graduated from Wharton. Yes, learning how to work hard gave my wife and me a nice living and a feeling of success. I made the transition, but teachers having pushed me more would have made the transition so much better. Maybe I would have learned how to study sooner, learned more, and not have struggled so hard."

Dorian Q.

Quality of Life

*"To awaken interest and kindle enthusi-
asm is the surest way to teach successfully."*

Tyron Edwards

"We come from the small village of Hopkins
in Belize. When we first had good schools, our
teachers had come to us through a program run
by the Belize government after World War II.
Because of the war many men were drafted into
the Army to fight in Europe and Africa. While
there, they received extensive training. Not
having much schooling themselves, the Army
taught them much knowledge and many new
skills. They were taught mathematics, science,
and other subjects. In order to fulfill their roles
in the Army they learned how to make roads,
construct bridges, and build buildings.

"When they returned from the war, the
country could not afford to pay them for their
war effort or to give them benefits. They could,
though, give them jobs as schoolteachers and an
assignment in a classroom. As it turned out this
was wonderful for Belize. It worked. These
men now knew discipline. They had also
learned geography, history etc., and had special
skills. I started school in 1963 and only went
through to the sixth grade, but I learned so much
from these teachers (this was true all over the
country). Our communities became our classrooms.
What they taught us in the classroom would
have some kind of application outside.

"We would learn some math and then take it outside and learn how to build something, maybe a small wooden bridge that wouldn't fall down like the old ones. At that time, in our village, we had no plumbing and we learned how to make quality pit latrines. (People who have never lived without plumbing wouldn't know, but this kind of knowledge leads to a real increase in the quality of living). When I left school I was fluent in English (my native languages are Guarifuna and Creole). I became a bridge builder, eventually started working in concrete and have now gained recognition across Belize.

"With time came retirements and then the new teachers, fully licensed, trained in education schools. This is when the problems started. These teachers only knew what was in the books. They could never say, 'I know it because I've done it,' they could only say, 'I know it because I've read it.'

"Students would only learn what they had to learn for the test, and teachers would only teach what they would test for. Everything was out of books. No more were the school children going out and learning in the community. They became bored, and the community changed.

"Hopkins is still a beautiful and special place. But now in our village you can see the difference between those people who had the Army teachers and those people who came after. It's a sparkle in the eye; it is the difference of motivation and the essence of feeling understood. If you don't have a teacher who has empathy for your life, it is harder to connect what you've learned to your life. Their empathy with your life helps give you the power to change your world."

Calvin N.

Did You Ever Have the

Power

the Teacher

Chapter Three

"Why is it when someone doesn't understand the words, the speaker just says them louder?"

Anonymous

Funny What You Can Learn if You Listen

Early on in my career I was teaching chemistry to a group of juniors. I was being very enthusiastic and particularly excited by the subject of the day. It was about how the attractive forces between water molecules affect so much of our world. I was drawing on the board and being very animated. At a certain point one of my students raised her hand, and after being called on, quietly offered the following: "Mr. Russell I can tell that you're very excited about what you're talking about and that's good," and then added, "but you don't have to yell."

How come I couldn't see that myself? It was so clear. I had been carrying on at the top of my lungs and I didn't have to. It is something I've seen with a number of teachers and it is on the list of student complaints. For some teachers it's just their particular presence. For others it's a way of rolling over the dull roar of students talking and passing notes. Perhaps it covers up their own insecurities. The loud volume is both uncomfortable and distracting. The group sigh of relief was palpable. It's funny, as soon as she said it to me, it was so obvious – I didn't have to be so loud. In fact a whole new way of interacting and of class management was opened to me by learning how to modulate and from discovering the power of quiet.

A Negotiated Settlement

*"I try never to let school get in the
way of my education."*
                              Mark Twain

Problems that arise in the classroom might be
due to a whole system not functioning properly.
The breakdown of the classroom, as a good place to
learn, can involve the entire school district, from
the students to the administration. Students benefit
from the proper balance of the exercise of
administrative authority and student empowerment.
When that balance is lost, no one is served well.
One can only imagine what Richard lost.

"When I finally got busted I had 69 absences.
    "Spring and fall? I couldn't resist those
nice days. In the winter when there was fresh
powder for downhill, the thought of school
just didn't fly. It was easy. I had a teacher
who never gave her papers back and rarely
gave tests back. She really knew her subject
and taught well, but really didn't prepare for
our classes. She knew that if she pushed us,
or tried to make us work we would say that
we wouldn't do anything unless we got our
stuff back. It was always kind of a joke but
kind of a deal we had worked out.
    "It was a check-mate sort of a situation.
You see, she couldn't send reports to the
office or home, that would start people looking too closely at her. And we didn't want to
complain about her, and have her be in

trouble with the administration. That would then wreck the whole deal. She was a very popular teacher, partly because what she was a good teacher and we did learn a lot. We also knew we didn't have to work very hard to get a good grade. If I didn't feel like coming to class, nothing was ever made out of it.

"It was a great 'negotiated settlement.' She didn't return our work, but always gave us an OK grade. We liked being in her class because it was fun and we didn't have to worry. She didn't bust us for not working or for ditching class and we stuck up for her if other people, parents or administrators, tried to take issue with her as a teacher. Good deal.

"After I got busted, they tried to fix it. It seemed to me that the administration was part of the problem too. I think they were being just like the teachers and not doing their job. The teacher deal can't happen if the teacher and the front office are all on the same page."

Richard P.

"P.S. Thankfully I graduated that year! I guess future students will have to renegotiate."

Elly K., age 6
Illinois, USA

A Coach for Life

"If you can dream it, you can do it."
Walt Disney

"My high school cross country coach was Doug Reid. This guy was quite a guy. He helped me believe in myself. In the ninth grade he seen me running and asked me to try out for track. I was smoking pot and being a 14 year old kid. My father became a Jehovah Witness and had thrown me out of the house. Well, Coach kept me in line and helped me realize that with a little hard work and some love, anything is possible. I loved running and I needed someone to show me how. But I didn't know that. But he believed in me, that I could run, and I was good. Well the next year I was on varsity track and running with the top guys in my field. In my junior year I had a cyst rupture in my femur. It stopped me from running for the whole year. Part of what helped me come back from that was because I wanted to run for the man who believed in me. We did good that next year, another great finish.

"When I left school, I turned down a scholarship for running. I thought it was time to go into the military. During my third year I had an accident when a five-ton truck lost control.

"It was hell because I lost all my memory and I had shattered my right elbow as well as injuring both knees. I went from a soldier to

Yorin B. age 4
Uitqeest, Netherlands

a cripple. I started putting pieces back and overcame many challenges – and when I could not, I learned to move on. It was because this man showed me how to believe in myself most of all. It took almost 10 years and still counting, changing my life. His simple belief in me made a whole lot of difference.

"I was just back home in Texas for my grandma's funeral. I stopped to see Coach at his home. It was nice to share with him what I felt: that he is a good man, and a great teacher. He got my younger twin brothers running and got them into college with running scholarships. That is a teacher loving, and looking out for all his kids.

"I have two kids of my own now and I try to instill that belief in them so they too can be able to continue even when they do not want to, because the reward of hard work pays off big. Believe me, I am proof of that. You would never know that I was disabled or that I lived the life I did, and went through what I did. But because a simple man believed in me, I learned to believe in myself and I know that whatever I do, as long as it is with love, I cannot fail. Love, faith and hope are strong things. Doug Reid, thanks a million, you gave me real power. That is my hero because he is still there riding his old bike, helping the kids today even though he is retired, living a modest life, happy being a coach… and look at me out here trying to live my dreams. And what a ride it has been, but hey, I am not stopping here, my ride has just began."

Mike N.

Coach's Story

*"Learning isn't compulsory...
neither is survival."*

W. Edwards Deming

Mike's "Coach for Life" story was about a "mentor" who helped him develop self-empowerment as a life-long skill . After reading Mike's story about his coach Doug Reid, I couldn't resist trying to reach Doug, as I had some other teachers. I found him in his hometown and called him. This is where he had been a coach. He had spent a lifetime as the boys' track coach at the local high school, having an impact on the kids who came through his program. As Mike had written, he was enjoying his retirement, although still semi-active.

A year after Doug retired, his high school renamed their relay race after him. It is now the "Doug Reid Relays." I told him about Mike's story and offered to send him a copy, which I did. He remembered Mike and reminisced a little. He also talked about how coaches are really teachers.

Of course they teach children about sports but they also teach children about working as a team and instill in them important values and life skills. So in the spirit of, *Did you ever have the teacher*, I asked him what had he learned from students that made him a better teacher. Was there a moment when he said to himself – "I do that and I don't have to?"

He said "Billy T." so quickly that it was obvious he had thought about this issue…

"The way I used to run practice was to spend a lot of time with these kids, early on in the school year, trying to instill in them a sense of teamwork, honesty, and hard work, to watch out for each other. The goal was to be there for each of them and help them become the best they could be. But I was hard on them. I would set them up in groups and have them practice and work out and I would go from group to group.

"If I came back to a group of boys who were not trying their hardest, who had gotten off 'track,' so to speak, I would be very hard on them and would really tear into them. I would get mad. I wasn't even aware of it, but I had developed a style of discipline that was completely contrary to what I wanted to accomplish.

"I was using my own power to disempower them, but I didn't know it. Well one day Billy T. asked if he could speak to me privately. 'Coach, when you get mad at us that way you make us really feel bad, not just about failing to try harder, but about ourselves. It's how you do it.'

"'In one outburst like that you destroy everything you had done to help us feel better about ourselves.' He showed a lot of emotion while he said this. It's odd but I could see that I had gotten caught up in this way of doing things. From then on I used a lot more humor and became much more supportive. There may be important things that happen here, but let's treat each other well."

                                                                Doug R.

Joel M., age 8
Texas, USA

Talking Hands

"I've learned that you can't go through life wearing a catcher's mitt on both hands, you need to be able to throw something back."

Maya Angelou

The next five stories are about the impact of the misuse of power by teachers and the feeling of the loss of power by students.

***

"Mostly my teachers were good. In the third grade I was a bright, animated young child that enjoyed participating in class. I was generally well liked by my teachers, as I looked forward to school and I loved learning. A characteristic of mine, though, was if I was speaking about something that I was very interested in I would sometimes 'talk with my hands' as well. For whatever reason this bothered my third grade teacher, Mrs. Wilcox.

"Eventually, one day after I had told my show-and-tell story to the class she said, 'Now, let's see if you can do that without using your hands.' She proceeded to hold my hands down on my desk and make me tell the story again. I felt like a trapped animal and I couldn't really do it. She was making me completely embarrassed. I tried my best to re-tell my story. Mrs. Wilcox was looking right in my face and the whole class was laughing at me. I have often remembered this humiliation over my years as a student, even through college. It led me to be more hesitant to share my thoughts or participate in class, something I began to do again only if I were completely comfortable.

"I have no idea what Mrs. Wilcox's motivation was, but, even though it was only the third grade, I think she abused her power as a teacher and had a detrimental effect on my whole education.

Erin W.

Princess and the Pee

"A teacher is one who makes himself
progressively unnecessary."

Thomas Carruthers

As in the last story, having power and using power are
two very different things. It seems that sometimes in the
exercise of power you can lose it, and also lose the respect
that might have come with it. There were lots of stories where
the bathroom was the issue. Not being able to take a pee
when you need to, seems to epitomize the issue of not having
power or personal choice. When someone else has control
over when you can go to the bathroom, it would be nice to
feel that you will be respected. This story had so much
character to it that I left it just as it was, so bear with the
writer. Not being allowed to pee is like being taken prisoner
and it permeates everything else you "rember about school."

Emma A., age 10
Kungsor, Sweden

"I had a teacher for the fifth grade. She was
a very awful teacher, she was a real peice of
crap, mean, and made learning a horabale
experiance, I would love for any one to hear
the awful story I have of that year Mrs.
McGrath what a hell year. I guess, I can
rember when they told us our teachers the
other kids saying oh no u got mcgraph, and
from there was a nightmare. Well the worst
thing I rember is she was very wierd about
going to the bathroom, in other words she would not let u go, but she was so
wierd, if u snezed she would make u go blow ur nose, but if u had to pee it
was no way. I can rember having to pee so bad and just holding it for hrs and
peeing my pants a little. It was horibal, thinking now I should have faked a
snezz but I was to honest and young, she allways gave you the hardest work
too, and did not do crap to help u, the old bat would just sit there scratching
her boob and reading, she was terable well…"

Cali W.

63

Long-term Effects

"The masters make the rules for the wise men
and the fools got nothing...to live up to."

Bob Dylan

From these last few stories, it seems likely that when a student
shares in the power over their education, they will be more open to
learning, will probably retain more, and are likely to feel that they
"own" it. Having no power leads to alienation, and alienation leads
to an adversarial relationship to education. A valuable source for
insight into what can go wrong for kids who have no power, is the
kid who ultimately fails out of regular high school. One such student,
Jon, asked me if he could share his story. I met him in his classroom,
and although very polite and respectful, his body language showed
that he carried a lot of angry feelings. He had learned from life to
be a tough kid on the outside, and now, as a senior in the "adult"
program, didn't care much for school, or teachers. Jon lost the
power over his education in first grade and never got it back.

He described how his first grade teacher
would let the class watch television every day
after lunch. He wanted to watch just like
everyone else did. He tried his hardest not to be
fidgety, to stay in his seat and not move. He just
couldn't.

"Every day I would get yelled at and then
separated from the other students. The teacher
would make me stand in the front corner of the
classroom with my nose touching the wall." This
was in full view of the other students who would
laugh at him. His back was to the rest of the class.

If he didn't keep his nose touching the corner he would be given an "after school assignment." As he got to this part you could see that he was starting to well up. He couldn't let himself cry.

After a moment, I asked him if he thought that his teacher's actions had any long-term effects. He glanced around as if to say, "Well, look where I am," and then, shrugging his shoulders, said, "Well, yeah!" I guess that was a silly question. He went on to add that no matter how he tried, he had a bad experience in every one of his classes. His expectations were that his new teacher would treat him like his first grade teacher did, and they did. "Where were the adults here"?

It tainted his outlook, and as a result he never felt part of his grade, and never felt connected with the other students. It is ironic that now that he is in a program where most of the students also felt mistreated, he finally feels like he belongs.

Tamislav P., age 12
Subatica, Yugo.

Narcissus 101

*"So may he love himself, and
not gain the thing he loves."*

Ovid

Narcissism and power go hand-in-hand. Narcissists have an inflated view of their talents and abilities, and everything is all about them. When they have power, they use it for themselves and don't care much about others. It is not that unusual therefore that we find narcissists as teachers. In response, students might say, "he was just so full of himself." The problem seems to be that teachers who are self-centered spend a lot of time convincing the class of how smart they are, even if they fail to educate the student. It is very seductive to use the "bully pulpit" of teaching to solicit the adulation of students, even if for many narcissists it is filling a bottomless pit of self-gratification.

Felipe B., age 10
San Paulo, Brazil

"We were all in class for the first day of Psychology. As often happens on the first day, we spent a little time getting to 'know each other.' The odd thing about this class though, is that after each person spoke the teacher would tell a story about himself; almost as if to one-up the student. After he got class started he began to describe how the class would go. With each aspect he would outline, he would add on something more about what he thought or believed, or what he had studied in college (and how well he had done). He even told us all about his family. 'Oh well,' I thought, maybe he wants a less formal class environment. But it didn't stop. If you tried to offer something about yourself he almost seemed impatient. Well, that was the class…

"Our first assignment was to go online and read a certain website. He gave us the address. To my amazement it was his web site. It was dedicated to his whole life, everything he had done and how good it all was: his childhood, his schooling, his friends, everything. There was a lot of personal detail and intimate stuff, along with his life history. We had to read his personal website and learn all about him.

"The next day when we came back to class he gave us a quiz! He actually quizzed us on whether we had read his website and whether we knew enough about him to his satisfaction. I really couldn't believe this. I was mad. I wanted to escape. How dare he take advantage of us, abusing our innate trust, especially on our first day? Every student wants to be accepted and nobody would have had the where-with-all to stand up to his self-serving behavior. For the remainder of the year, psychology was all about him. Teachers can do weird things but, I think that what this teacher did was empty, selfish, unfair, and narcissistic."

Sonya T.

Catholic Stutterer

*"I am both blind and I stutter, but stuttering
has been worse to deal with than blindness
because people just don't understand stuttering."*
                                                    Eric Warren

---

"Being a freshman at an 'all-girls' Catholic high school
was challenging. In addition, I also had a moderately
severe stuttering problem. As a result I kept pretty quiet
in class. One day, with about 20 minutes left in the class,
my German language teacher asked me to stand up and
give a verbal response. I tried but I was unable to reply
due to the tension I felt and the fear of stuttering.

"She was not even asking me a question to test my
knowledge – it was just a 'repeat after me' exercise, but
I was unable to answer.

"To make things worse the teacher said, 'Well,
I guess we'll all just sit here and wait for Jessica to
answer.' I kept getting stuck on the first word. I felt
completely powerless. My mind was in a panic.

"She made the class sit there. The teacher, with her
arms folded in front of the class, made me stand at my
desk. I felt complete, silent, humiliation. The rest of the
class was uncomfortable and shuffling – until the bell
rang. We were finally released.

"I have worked myself through my stuttering difficulties
over time. People who don't stutter can't understand the
impact this condition has on your life. With compassion
and understanding from those whose job it is to help,
stuttering can be, in some cases, overcome. But instead,
she used her power to traumatize me.

"I sought help for my stuttering. When I would work at
keeping my words coming, I would often visualize the moment
in this class where I was standing there, scared and unprotect-
ed, and the stuttering would start up. I have never understood
what good she thought would come from what she did."

                                                    Jessica D.

Afghan Woman

*"Calling someone from Afghanistan an 'Afghani'
is like calling someone from America a 'Dollar.'
The 'Afghani' is the Afghanistan currency"*
                                    An Afghan Vendor

I met this woman when going in for a haircut. She
was a little over fifty, regal and confident in a self-
effacing way. She, as usually happens when getting a
haircut, asked me what I do. I explained to her about
this book. She suggested that school for her was very
different than for American children. Her story
exposes the conflict between the use of power for
control and classroom discipline vs. respect and the
freedom to be creative. It helps give a little perspective.

Lucia W., Age 5
Frankfurt, Germany

"Born in Afghanistan in 1953, I began
school at the elementary level when I was
six. This was also the first year women
were admitted to the schools or university. Our classes were very disciplined.
You would no more dare to speak out in
class or at your teacher than you would
swear at your parents. We were all very
well behaved; there were no 'bad children.' We were too afraid to misbehave.

"As is often true in America, our
elementary classes were all in one room,
with one teacher. Our teachers were
not accustomed to having girls in their
school. They were very mean to us.
They never said anything to support us
and always made us feel bad. As an
example, although we spoke Pashto,

we were required to recite Farsi poetry in class. These poems were considered important. I can't say why, as we never learned what any of them meant. But we would be asked to stand in front of the class and recite them from memory. I hated that. Inside yourself, before you spoke, you would be afraid because you knew no matter how hard you would try, the teacher would ridicule you in front of the other students, and tell you how poor a job it was. He would grab hold of your ear and push his fingernail into it and then pull you. And afterwards, you would always want to cry. At home there was no support from your family because there was nothing they could do.

"Another frustration was that your grade was based on what the teacher felt like giving you. This power over grading lasted all the way through school. It felt as though they would determine how successful you were by what they thought of you and what your family 'deserved' and that was the grade you got. Teachers had a lot of control over who you were allowed to become. When I went to high school my teachers would give me whatever grade they thought appropriate; it may or may not have been a reflection of what I had earned. Their decision about what you received was absolute and you could not change it even if your work deserved better.

"We would study many courses each year. We studied everything. We took full courses, for example, economics, geography, statistics, geology, English, every area. We had more subjects than students would have to study in the States. Each year starting in the ninth grade we had at least seven courses.

"If you did not pass every single class, if you failed one course, you would be held back to repeat the entire year. You had to take all the courses, not just the ones you failed but the ones you passed, as well. If one teacher did not like you or chose to fail you, even though you had worked hard and had mastered all the courses, you were forced to have the humiliation of repeating the year. There was no happiness in learning, you were powerless in every aspect of your life.

"Living in the United States now is interesting because I see in American children behaviors that would never have been tolerated in Afghanistan. These behaviors would be considered to be social decline and would have been unacceptable. On the other hand there is a level of creativity of thought and power over one's own destiny that exists here that could never have existed there. There was no respect for Afghan students, they were powerless. At least there is the possibility of more than that here.

"My husband and I left Afghanistan to come here in 1999. Now people always say to me, 'Aren't you lucky to have gotten out of Afghanistan with the Taliban in power, and before the US invasion.' I remind them that, yes we got out during the oppresion of the Taliban, but not before living through the occupation by the Russians, the military take-over, the communist coup, etc. Afghanistan is a beautiful but difficult place. Isn't it remarkable now to be a well educated, intelligent woman, living in America. I am grateful.

Shahida B.

Who's Being Protected...?

"Boundaries define limits and mark off dividing lines. The purpose of a boundary is to make clear separations."

Robert Burney

This story, from a recent high school graduate, is appropriate for the transition from consider power into exploring the issue of boundaries. We often think we are using the power of the system to help protect our students. But are we? It is important to remember what it is that we are trying to do. Perhaps without paying attention we might sometimes lose view of our goal and violate student boundaries rendering them powerless.

"It was the spring, I was a junior in high school and was sitting in Mrs. Atherton's room taking a pre-calculus midterm. The school secretary came over the intercom, 'Mrs. Atherton, we'd like to see Cindy Lansing.' Mrs. Atherton protested, stating that I was in the middle of an exam, but 'the office' was not concerned with my exam. I began to worry. My grandfather had just had a heart attack. I thought for sure something was horribly wrong at the hospital. By the time I got to the office I had convinced myself that 'Papa's dead.'

"I walked into the principal's office to find Sally Pittston, an English teacher popular for having slept with the former principal and for smoking pot with her students. Also, of course, the new principal, Mr. Chase was there, with whom, up until now, I had no problems; and the superintendent, Agnus Oxnard, a woman of whom the mere thought still conjures up adrenaline I often forget I have.

"This cast of characters did not seem the appropriate committee to tell me news about my grandfather, but this thought did not alleviate the fear building in my seventeen-year-old chest.

"I sat, as I was instructed to do; and then the questions started. 'Do you know why you are here?' 'Do you know that we have information about an affair between you and a teacher?' 'Have you ever had a boyfriend your own age?' 'How often do you sleep with older men?'

"It took awhile to find my bearings; then I became angry. Mr. McAllister was a teacher that I admired a great deal. He was also the cause of insecurity for other teachers because of his unusual and successful teaching methods, but was alienated by the administration because of his closeness with students. There had been rumors about him and other girls every year since his divorce. I was not surprised that I was next on the list. We were close and often talked. He was more than just a teacher to me, he was also a friend. Even with these past rumors, which also were not true, I had never heard anything about any kind of interrogation. This all surprised me.

"I learned later that they had interrogated one of my friends before even calling me in. They had asked her questions about me, my sex life, what I talked about, where I went, when I 'went out,' who I hung out with. She knew exactly what they were getting at and she, thinking that it would help, went and warned many of my friends who were in the art-room during my interrogation.

"By the time I got out of my first interrogation the whole school knew. About 50 feet out of the office Billy G. yelled over to me, 'So how is he Cindy? Is he good?' In just getting to my car, a fair number of similar comments had been made. My car was surrounded by the boys in my grade as well as the senior class. They were all shouting comments about my 'affair' as I drove away. I guess I would have been excited and curious about such a scandal too, had I been on the outside of it.

"The administration was falsely accusing him. The false accusation originated from a student who had only just become a student of his. She was sitting in Mr. McAllister's room one afternoon, playing music and singing, as students often did with him. I went in to pick up any assignments I had missed. We were friendly and apparently the girl assumed there was something going on between us. She turned it into an accusation with the one teacher who everyone knew could not stand Mr. McAllister (because of his success), remember Sally Pittston, who promptly escorted her to the principal. He made a call to the superintendent.

"My parents had no idea what was going on, and I went to the hospital and sat quietly with my grandfather trying to imagine where this whole thing was going. I was interrogated for the next two days, off and on. I left school whenever I wanted for the most part; I think the school knew that what they were doing was wrong. They were not going to harass me about going for a drive to smoke a cigarette, if that is

what it took to keep me calm. I ended up
crashing my car in the days that followed. I was
upset and speeding into town to catch up with a
friend who had more to tell me about who the
administration was interrogating.

"Mr. McAllister left the school, having made
an arrangement with the school district that they
pay him the following year's salary and there
would be no negative impact on his record.
I was left feeling guilty; this man lost his job for
being a friend to me.

"What are the problems with this picture?
Mr. McAllister had no protection. Despite the
lack of evidence and denial of the accusations
on all fronts, he was left without recourse for
the damage done by these false accusations.
Although he was being falsely accused, there
was no clear way for Mr. McAllister to bring
any action against them.

"The rumor and accusations never made it
into the local media; therefore he would not
have even had the classic remedy of claiming
defamation. And who was looking out for my
interests; not their interests about me, but my
interests? My parents did not know what was
going on until 3 or 4 days after the interrogations
started, and aside from that, they are not well
educated and would never have thought of
bringing a lawsuit. The school administrators
were attacking me. I felt like the system,
instead of helping me, left me with nothing.
Who was actually protected here?"

Cindy S.

Did You Ever Have the Teacher

Boundaries

Chapter Four

"Preconceived notions are the locks on the door to wisdom".

Merry Browne

Not Enough Space...

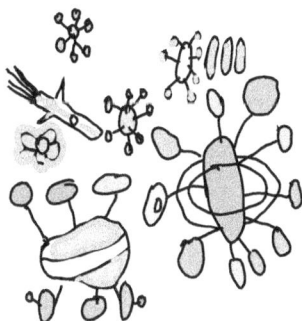

It was clear that my students would rather talk about outer space than memorize boring historical facts about how molecules work and what they are made of. That was easy, I went with outer space. I decided to "explore" the origin of the universe with them – get into the good stuff first. What is space? Go past the planets. Are there really black holes, and the fourth dimension? All the stuff they love to talk about. As we were going farther into space, we were discussing things that occurred further back in time, until you eventually arrive at the beginning of time. How intriguing.

Perched at the beginning of time, the

beginning of everything, it was hard not to ask, from a scientific point of view, how did the universe come into existence? Describing how the universe exploded into existence allowed me to talk about the particles – quarks and bosons, then protons and neutrons, and electrons, coming into existence. It became "easy" to see how they came together to make atoms and molecules and begin to predict why they do what they do, in other words - chemistry...

We spent a week taking this journey, and I was proud of how it went and how engaged the students were. The idea seemed to be working wonderfully. But, at the end of all this one of my students came to me in tears. "Mr. Russell, I don't know what to do. I trust you but what you're telling me is contrary to everything that my family ever told me about the world."

She then went on to tell me that her family has taught her to believe that the universe is only 6000 years old, or so. It is one thing to talk about science that is here-and-now, the kind of stuff you can put your hands on, but to talk about where it all came from, that's different. That's the realm not just of science but also of religion. She was in a real quandary. So was I, and didn't know what to do. We sat down together and I tried to reassure her. "It might help to look at this as just one way of thinking, and keep all your ways of thinking open. Use it, but don't just accept it. It is some more information to help you think and figure out what the truth is for yourself." I felt really bad that this poor girl was in such turmoil because of what she was learning in my classroom.

I felt that I had failed to protect a boundary, that I hadn't properly invited her into the discussion. In fact, teaching in a public school, I became concerned. I went to the principal and told him the story in hopes of gaining some insight into how best to handle the problem. He just shook his head and added, "I don't think anyone's going to be able to help you. Her father is a closed minded fundamentalist preacher, with very specific ideas of what's 'true'." That gave me great solace…

Not sure what to do, I went right to my dcsk and called him up. I figured it was better that I call him than have him come looking for me. I just said, "I have to tell you what happened today with your daughter and I'm really calling you to ask for your advice on how I should handle it." I explained the whole week to him and how his daughter had responded and I told him about our conversation. To my surprise, he was quite happy about it all. I was expecting to get run out of town, but instead he said, "No, it is good for her to have this exposure, she can learn what other people are thinking about 'out there.' With my help she will realize that it's wrong and there is really only our one way to look at it. Keep up the good work."

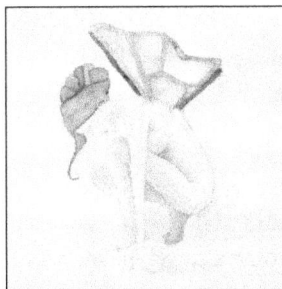

Brynn S., age 12
Florida, USA

Don't Call Me Out ...

"And this is one of the major questions of our lives: how we keep boundaries, what permission we have to cross them, and how we do so."

A. B. Yehoshua

I remember a Biology teacher in the room next to mine who was always out in the hall having an argument with some student. As soon as he got "down" to the same level as the student, he had crossed a boundary and no longer had the students' respect. He took things personally and it usually ended in the student being sent to the office. Some teachers will get into big arguments with students over small discipline issues. Once a teacher "gets into it" with a student, the teacher loses – and students know it.

I had a group of kids one day that were doing their best to behave but were finding it a little "challenging." One student was pushing the edges with me and needed to be "encouraged" to calm down. I interrupted him, and class, with a short, friendly, but direct comment, instructing him that he was a little out of line and needed to straighten up. It was not angry or confrontational, but was done in front of the whole class. After school he came by and offered some insight into how to make things better for him.

He explained that as a matter of pride. Should a teacher get mad at a student, like him, in front of his friends, he would have to stand up to it. It is better to have an argument, no matter the consequences, than to let it look as if the teacher is getting the best of him in front of others. He was trying to tell me that students don't always argue with the issue, they mind having it happen in a way that embarrasses them in front of their peers. Getting into "his space" was crossing a boundary. He wanted me to know that he would deal with anything, and respond to whatever discipline issue came up, as long as the teacher didn't do it in front of everyone. If it has to be done in front of the class then crack a little joke, something that he and the others can laugh at, but not feel any humiliation; or come over to the table and whisper something. "Let me know that there is a problem privately – don't call me out."

Here is a story about how a teacher who used this idea. No boundaries were crossed. He used a gentle touch, a little humor and subtle discipline. Confrontation was avoided and a sense of camaraderie remained within the classroom.

––––––––––––––––––

"English class had started. It was just after lunch. I was sitting in my seat in the back of the classroom next to this girl. All of a sudden her cell phone goes off. Everyone looks to the back of the room. Quickly she pushes some buttons and it stops ringing. It became clear a few moments later that she hadn't shut the ringer off because it began ringing again. She goes through the same routine. Now in our school cell phones are strictly forbidden in the classroom, even though everyone brings them. The class was fairly tense about what would happen. Finally, on the third time, she ducks down behind her desk, brings the phone up to her face and answers it.

"She said, in a whisper – you know the kind that everyone can hear – 'You're kidding! You mean that's why you're calling me? All you want to know is *where I'm at*? Stop it, I'm in class!'

"It's at this point the teacher walks to the back of the classroom, right up to her desk, and in a stern voice says: 'Leslie!' She looks up at the teacher, 'That's wrong, just plain wrong' The rest of the class is silent. He leans forward, looking at her, and says, 'In the future say, '*where I am*, *where I'm at* is redundant. Now please put the cell phone away.' And with a smile the whole situation was diffused. On the way out of class he called her over and I'm sure they had a little discussion about what had happened. The cool thing though is instead of a big blowout in class, there was no confrontation, nobody getting into each other's space, and class was actually more of a group. Just thought you might like to have a story about how things can be done right."

Andrew P.

81

Science Fair?

"The stumbling blocks in the way of grasping the truth are: weak and unworthy authority, longstanding custom, and the hiding of our own ignorance while making a display of our apparent knowledge."

Roger Bacon

"Science teachers are a problematic lot. For some people science is one of those subjects that is just difficult to get, and boring to listen to. I was one of them. But nonetheless science teachers are given a certain special status because they are assumed to know things about how the natural world works that others don't. What seems the most unfair though is that if we can't learn we often blame ourselves and not the teacher's inability to teach. It's as if to say, 'my science teacher was so smart I just couldn't understand him.'

"By placing themselves above you, they create a boundary that keeps you away from them and keeps you from learning. Einstein once said, 'you don't really understand something well enough until you can explain it to your grandmother.' I wish that was what my science teacher could have done, then I could have asked my grandmother. If they can't explain it simply, then they don't understand it well enough to be teaching it. I want my science teacher to have the capacity to give the content to me in a form that I can learn, and then to change that form to help someone with different difficulties.

"I think some teachers get filled with the idea that they know a whole lot more than they really do. They like the admiration and respect they are given for appearing to be knowledgeable; smarter than they really are. As a result they start giving answers, advice, and especially opinions, they really don't have the right to give. I think that's true of many teachers, not just science teachers.

"Science teachers intimidate kids. Perhaps they allow their students to be intimidated to cover their insecurity about their lack of knowledge. It seems to me that when a teacher uses their inequality to intimidate and gain admiration at the expense of students, they necessarily fail to teach. The teacher is to blame.

"My ninth grade science teacher led us to believe that he knew everything. And we believed whatever he said. He used to say aliens from outer space caused life to occur on Earth and made things like the 'crop circles' in England. I thought that was cool and would tell people about it. In looking back I feel like I lost something.

"He taught us that microwaves cook from the inside out. He used this 'fact' to explain that if you put a cat in the microwave it would explode. Why would he tell us about that – ugh. I have since learned that it is not true. Microwaves cook where the moisture is. I think my understanding of the world went backwards that year. Don't say something unless you know it with certainty. I am still confused about some things because of him.

"Yes, teachers like to seem smarter than students, and sometimes, when they are barely a step ahead of the students, the students don't learn much. It seems OK with the teacher, to maintain that aura of supposed intelligence and authority even at such a cost. And when I hear some people talk about how wonderful their science teacher was and how much it has meant in their lives, I know they exist, I just wish I had had one of them."

James W.

For Better or Worse

"Art is either plagiarism or revolution."
Paul Gauguin

Trust and boundaries are closely connected issues. You violate the first one and you may well cross or create the second. The remainder of this chapter explores the consequences of not honoring boundaries on the one hand, and creating them on the other.

"College had just started. I was a freshman and it was my first semester English class. We had been reading about 'Oedipus' and 'Antigone' and the Greek tragedies, and had to write a paper about them. For whatever reason, these stories are very popular in English classes, and it was my third time studying the tragedies.

"I remember working really hard on this one particular paper since I felt fairly comfortable with the material. I wrote up an outline and a rough draft, then typed and edited it over a period of a week-and-a-half (more time than I had spent on most papers in my college career). It was one of the few times I remembered enjoying the process of writing a paper. It was also an important paper and many of us were anxious for the results.

"The time came for the professor to hand back our papers. Instead, in class, she informed us that she believed that one of us had plagiarized their paper and until that person came forward, she wouldn't be handing them back.

"I thought it was strange, and kind of felt sorry for the person who thought they had no other choice but to use someone else's work in order to get by. My friends and I talked about how bad it must feel to be this person and know that you are busted and it is only a matter of time.

"After a week, no one had come forward. She relented and said we could pick up our papers in the English office. I went to get mine and when I didn't see it with the rest, I thought 'Oh s**t!' I started to feel nauseous and panicky. I went to the professor's office down thc hall. She looked like she had been expecting me.

"At this point I was fully aware that she believed I plagiarized my paper. It was an awkward conversation. My head was spinning and I don't recall the details too much except that I felt trapped. How was I going to prove I didn't copy it? What if I couldn't prove that I had written my own paper? That is the sort of thing that would get you expelled at my school.

"What I do remember her saying was that she thought I had plagiarized my paper because it was so much better than the last couple of papers I did. Hey, wow – thanks. I improve my writing and I'm accused of copying someone else's work?

"Fortunately, I had kept my written rough draft and showed that to her, with my resources and all the work I had put into it. She mostly avoided me after that incident. I think she ended up giving me a B on the paper, but it always seemed unfair. I never felt fully trusted after that. There was now a boundary that made me feel like an outsider and less welcomed in her class."

Jenna J.

Plagiarism

"Pereant qui ante nos nostra dixerent."
("Perish those who said our good things before we did.")
Aelius Donatus

For six years I helped the yearbook club produce the yearbook. Sometime in the spring, we would send the last proofs, the corrected pages, and changed photographs irretrievably off to the printer. Then after that, of course, we had to deal with Annie's crisis pleading with us, although it was too late, to please get "Mikie's name out of my yearbook page because my new boyfriend, Frankie, will never forgive me when he reads what I wrote." After all that, we would start the process of picking the new editor.

Usually the applicants for editor were juniors or seniors, but this year among the applicants were two tenth grade girls applying as co-editors. In order to evaluate the applicants, as standard fare in these kinds of things, I would have them write an essay about why they wanted the position. Among these essays were their absolutely outstanding and beautifully written pieces. How could these two tenth graders have written such fine work. It seemed improbable to me.

I spoke with their teachers. That didn't much help. "Great kids, extremely capable, but with very pushy parents." Their English teacher thought their essay had some outside help. I wrestled with it for a while and came to the conclusion that there was too great a likelihood that these students hadn't actually done the writing. I had become the gatekeeper.

Perhaps they had their parents craft the essays and then they copied them. I didn't know, but I had too many doubts, and although I never accused them, I didn't pick them for the role.

The next year I had them both in my Chemistry class. As I got to know these girls I realized that they were very bright, creative, independent and motivated young ladies. I am certain, now, that I was wrong. The work they did for me in chemistry made it very clear that they not only wrote their own essays but also would have followed through on their vision for the yearbook. By my decision, I created a boundary that prevented them from an educational experience they deserved. Since then I have a default position about assumption of authorship. I will assume that the work is original unless I have very substantive reasons for thinking otherwise. Being accused of plagiarism is a deeply undermining experience that has real consequences, as we read in the following story...

_____

"When I was maybe in fifth grade, I was in an advanced English class. It made me feel separated from the other students. I already was finding myself different from most of the children at this particular suburban Philly school. First of all, I came from a single parent home with a mother who worked round the clock. It wasn't like that for the other students. I felt like an outcast. Mayville residents surrounded me.

"I found myself often filled with musings about the Mayville residents and from those feelings, I wrote a poem. I felt really good about it.

Some of the vocabulary may have seemed a little beyond my age, yet I never thought that it would lead to what happened. I guess it was beyond what the teacher thought was possible from a student of hers.

"Yet nonetheless, I had a solid enough understanding of the words to write it and I considered it to be a pretty good poem. I remember it was called 'Pen and Paper' and dealt with my observations of the world around me. I felt it had significance as something seen through the eyes of a girl. But after she read it, she looked at me and ripped it up, slowly, right in front me. As she ripped it up she ridiculed me. She yelled at me and accused me of plagiarism. I was being accused of having plagiarized my own creation. I was devastated.

"Even now, the pain of my creative spirit being crushed by someone is still there. Apparently she had her own issues – or own blindness – her own 'bad teaching' habits – and the effect was left with me, and made me feel that I was more of an outsider than ever. I couldn't even trust my teacher..

"Never doubt – always believe – because as teachers – you are the ones who inspire – who enlighten – who care – who guide and who are supposed to believe. You chose your path – it is a precarious one, with a lot of influence, so be careful."

Colleen

Claire J. age 7
Paris, France

Favoritism

"My teachers could have easily ridden with Jesse James for all the time they stole from me."

Richard Brautigan

We require students to maintain boundaries; do we ask the same of ourselves.? Do we unthinkingly enter someone's "space," and cause them to become uncomfortable, or do we, unknowingly, create a "space" into which only some are allowed? These issues might arise because of teachers showing preferences, having inappropriate relationships that give special access, or by taking advantage of students. In other words just plain crossing boundaries. As with so many stories, we hear how the proper respect for boundaries is a fundamental ingredient of the good teacher. The result of behavior that violates students' boundaries is a sense of isolation, a loss of power, and a feeling of doubt about one's self-worth. Not being sensitive to students' boundaries is perhaps the most serious mistake a teacher can make, because it involves trust, control, and the power to humiliate. The loss of certainty about their boundaries results in not knowing if they are safe and of not having fair access to their teacher (and a good education). No one has the right to take that away.

———————

"Who plays favorites … I had a high school history teacher who was obviously playing favorites with the more popular students, particularly the pretty girls. If one of the regular kids came into class late, he would mark them late and sometimes send them to the office to get a pass. This of course made them later and they missed more class. Lots of times when he sent one of the students to the office for being late he wouldn't have even started class yet. He would be sitting there talking with the 'girls.' If one of the pretty girls came in late he would joke with them about 'so what were you girls up to?' as if he knew some inside info that they shared.

"The thing that was so obvious to the rest of us is that these girls flirted with him just to 'dupe' him and get away with whatever they could. They had little 'in-jokes' with him and the girls would say things that lead him to actually think he had a 'chance.' Then outside of class, you couldn't believe the awful things they would say about him.

"He was completely available to those girls but not to the rest of us. When he ran class he would hang out in their part of class. It really felt bad. He made us feel as if we couldn't approach him because we weren't the special ones. I know that my education was not as good as it could have been because I felt like such an outsider in that class. He made me feel like I was an annoyance. It felt easier sometimes to just not try. If you had a question on a test – well forget it – he would just say, 'you need to study more.' If one of the 'girls' asked him, he would give them hints. I used to listen in, hoping I could pick up some 'scraps.'

"There was one test that I thought I did very well on, but when I got it back I had a 'D'. I compared the answers with one of the special students and some of my 'wrong' answers were correct. However his mind worked, he figured he could give me fewer points. The only thing I could do was to try to be bold and confront him. He corrected it, giving me a B instead, but he didn't like it. I embarrassed him. He ended up giving me a 'D' in the class. He just made it up. I deserved much better.

The entire situation was a barrier that was put up for me and I was never allowed inside.

"I always did well in my other classes. I used my bad experience with this teacher as my college application essay. I was fortunate and was accepted into Yale. But this teacher made a terrible impression. He sure wasn't a good role model, and he wasn't fair on grading. I would hope that in the future some recourse is made available for situations like this. I remember that experience to this day and it still bothers me. It is easy to get caught up in it and at the time, I guess I felt jealous of those girls and wished I were 'cool.' Now though, I feel more angry at him; at his self-centeredness and what it took away from me.

"Favoritism exists in the real world and we have to learn to cope with it when it occurs. But it just should never be allowed into the classroom; the one place a student should feel safe from all that. As in my case, I have definitely experienced favoritism and have been affected by it.

Paul S.

Anna F., age 6
California, USA

Humiliation is...

"...Humiliation, ...is the square root of sin, as opposed to the freedom from humiliation, ...which is the square root of wonderful."
Carson McCullers

Humiliation is the boundary that should never be crossed. It robs a person of their dignity, lessens self-worth, and creates hatred.

———————————

"Humiliation is... a teacher that made an 8-year-old girl hate school. Teachers who have arbitrary rules and bring no fun into the classroom, can make every moment be filled with resentment. Can't they tell? They're not having any fun either.

"One day, we were reading the reader (forgot the full name). You know the idea though, those books you have to get and bring back to your seat and read. We were told, as always, that under no circumstances were we to speak or make any noise. She was like this with all the subjects and it made you hate anything she taught you. At the beginning I had to urinate and was in agony. I raised my hand and waved it; after all I couldn't say anything. I kept raising it, and she kept ignoring me. After a while I was frantic.

"I couldn't wait any longer and finally asked, out loud, if she would please let me go to the bathroom. But because I made a sound, she came over to me and pulled me out of the chair and spanked me. I couldn't hold it and wet my pants. Then she made me stand, in front of the whole class, next to the heater while my urine soaked clothes dried, and told the class what happened.

I was so humiliated. I cried all the way home from school and that night too.

"My parents were out of town and there was a baby sitter taking care of us. She knew something was wrong when I came home upset, but thought I was missing my parents. When I explained that wasn't it and I told her what happened, she really understood. She helped me clean up and she soothed my soul. The next day she took me to school and marched in to the principal's office and let them have it. To our surprise the teacher was suspended for a short time and I was placed in a different class. I was so happy to not have to see her again. All the students felt that way. She had used these tactics for a long time and no one had ever complained. It seemed she took pleasure in humiliation.

"I still feel the misery of that day. This teacher used her power to abuse me, but I felt that I learned about just-power with how it turned out."

Joyce V.

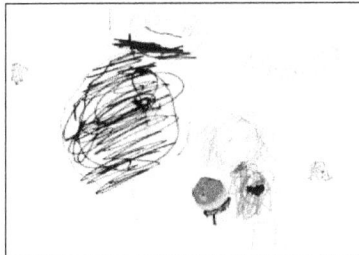

Carolina G., age 4
Buenos Aires, Argentina

The View Within

"Teachers are responsible for recognizing in themselves whether they are 'at risk' of crossing boundaries and, if they are, of addressing the issue. This makes the issue an important and dangerous one for them."

Elementary Teachers' Federation of Ontario

"There is probably no issue more important to maintain an awareness of, than boundaries. These last several stories really expose the alienation that occurs when boundaries are not honored. Favoritism, false accusations, and humiliation are all ways of crossing them. When boundaries are respected and access equal, trust can be built, a teacher's power can be used justly, and a learning environment, free of humiliation, can be established.

How does one know if they are within proper professional boundaries? If a teacher's actions aren't appropriate for all students, and if the potential benefit isn't available to everyone, then boundaries are not being honored. If a behavior is for some personal gain or gratification, and not targeted directly for students' benefit, then a boundary is being created. And if somehow the teacher allows some students to have special access, then a fair education is being denied for the others. As we have seen in other stories, like *Talking Hands* (p 62), and *Long-term Effects* (p 64), or as we will read in *A Separate Piece* (p 126), boundaries are violated by either going where a teacher shouldn't go, or keeping students away from what they should be given.

Boundaries work in three dimensions:

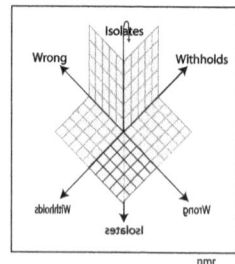

1) doing something to or with someone that is inappropriate or illegal,
2) doing something to someone that alienates them from their education, and,
3) treating some as special. This alienates others from having access to their teacher and their education. Access must be equal.

Each one of these will have aspects of the others, but fundamental to all three are disempowerment and the failure to provide a fair education.

94

Space Invaders

"Education is the ability to listen to almost anything without losing your temper or your self-confidence."

Robert Frost

"Being a shy kid made things difficult. I hated being the center of attention at school or wherever I was. I always tried to fade into the woodwork. I generally sat in the back of class so I wouldn't have to talk in front of everyone. For some reason I sat up in the front of the class this day. Let me describe what it is like to have had the 'space invader' teacher; the one who just gets into your space when you ask a question.

"I raised my hand. The teacher came over by my desk to answer. He leaned towards me and put his hands on my desk, looking right at me. His face felt like it was a foot away from mine. It was way too close for me, I could see the details of his face. I was really uncomfortable. I didn't even remember what I asked, and I had absolutely no idea what he was saying. Inside my head is 'go away, I'm sorry I opened my mouth, I promise I'll never do this again.' He was just too close. He talked on and on, (well it seemed like a long time), right in my face.

"When he was finished he stood up and looked at the class and, looking back at me asked, 'Does that answer your question?' The feelings inside of me were all over the place. I'm thinking – 'No, I didn't understand anything because you were right in my face making it impossible.' What I'm wanting to say is 'I hate you', 'go away,' 'I'll never ask you another question ever.' I could feel my face flush - and I just said - '*yes*'... He probably thought he had done a great job.

"I remember nodding, just hoping he would move away and stop talking to me. I was lying just to get the whole thing to stop. He had no idea what was going on inside of me. It took a few more years and a teacher I had more faith in, before I tried that again."

David R.

Did You
Ever Have
the
Teacher

Expectations

Chapter Five

"It is the supreme art of the teacher to awaken joy in creative expression and knowledge."

Albert Einstein

How Do We Know What We Know?

My students came tumbling into physics class from their first period class – it was April 1st. "Come on Mr. Russell, it's April Fools Day." They were all laughing. "Do your practical joke. We're ready for you," although it wouldn't be quite what they expected.

I hadn't realized it was April Fools Day, but decided on the spot to play along. I dismissed their challenges and told them that we had new material to work on. "We're starting a new section on sound," I told them, "and we need to get serious."

To my surprise they got ready to work, took out their notebooks and began to take notes. They copied down the illustrations from the board, and made calculations. Even though I seemed energetic and sounded sincere, the lecture was completely bogus.

"First, you need to know that sound is made up of small particles called beats." That didn't sound too far fetched. I explained that "when sound is emitted these beats travel through space into three-dimensional tubes called 'tubules'" – total nonsense. "They are everywhere but we can't see them" – no one question-ed me. "When sound occurs, beats are emitted and enter a tubule. I was scrambling for words...

"… and through an opening called a cannula."
I was just making it up as I went along. The
students seemed interested. They wrote things
down and asked questions. "Mr. Russell, are all
the beats the same or are they different for different
sounds?" I assured her I would answer later.
I continued. "The beat travels through the tubule
and comes out the other side." I drew a picture on
the blackboard to show how they came out of the
tubule. Now how was I going to get out of this?

"As each beat exits they shred little fibers off
of the tubule. The fibers slow down the beats and
trap them." I drew little lines showing the pieces
of tubule floating in space with a couple of beats
being trapped. Hmm… now I've got it. As my
picture progressed it looked perhaps a little like
musical notes and maybe a G-clef.

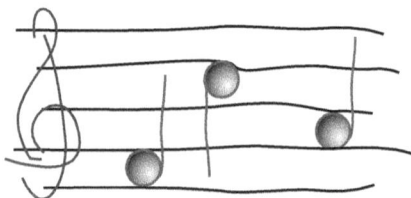

The kids continued to ask questions. But as my 'musical staff' became more evident, one student cried out: 'Oh no, it's all bulls**t.' There was a group gasp, and then a brief silence before everyone started laughing. Still, there was an undercurrent of disbelief. It was *funny*, kind of, but they couldn't believe that I had lied to them. They had spent eleven years in school and now a seed of doubt had been planted – what was true?

This led us to take a little departure for the week, one that had a positive result. They were clearly shaken, so we entered into a discussion about "How do we know what we know." We studied how learning had taken place over the millennia, how things have become known with "certainty" only later to be modified because they were found to be flawed. We explored how to be a receptive, but responsible and skeptical learner.

For my part, one expectation I should have of myself is to help provide a learning experience that contains the freedom to learn and the joy of critical thinking. Don't abuse the learner's trust. When the information they are getting is going to be false, invite them, early on, to discover the inconsistencies, don't just let them end up feeling embarrassed or stupid.

My April Fools Day lesson had backfired, which became very apparent in May when we studied sub-atomic Physics. I tried to explain such things as bosons, quarks and hadrons. The kids put their pencils down and revolted. "Oh yeah, sure" – closing their notebooks. "No really – I'm serious this time," I said, laughing.

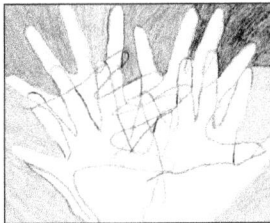

Harley D., Age 10
California, USA

The Buck Stops Here?

"If you can't explain it simply you don't understand it well enough."

Albert Einstein

It is not unusual for kids to have word problems for math in middle school. "The hardest thing about doing word problems is taking the English…and translating it into math… getting the equation can seem nearly impossible."* No wonder some students begin to hate math. Whatever it is that happens to kids with math between the fifth and eighth grades, though, is very real. It is all too common that students who had a good relationship with math up to the fifth grade, go through a transformation in middle school and lose their confidence. They develop that mental noise that keeps them from thinking.

I have worked with many kids as juniors and seniors who would say that they "used to be really good at math." There is something we do in how we teach that has a negative impact on kids and their math, particularly girls. Perhaps if we just listened we might hear how to teach to them differently. It is reasonable that students expect us to understand them. Maybe if we tried to think like they do, we might be able to.

"**Y**a I did…. Mrs. Buck, at my middle school:

"She taught a pre-algebra class I was in. Like a lot of kids I just couldn't get word problems. I was not able to understand how you looked at a word problem and then, from the words, set up the problem and somehow got the X (the unknown). When she tried to explain it, it was like listening to a rocket scientist.

"She was not capable of dumbing it down enough for me to understand. She even went so far as to say something to the effect, 'it's so obvious, it doesn't get

* Purplemath.com

100

any simpler than that.' Imagine how that felt. To an adolescent eighth grader it was pretty uncool. I know that if she had used the right level of teaching and support, and helped me along, I could have mastered it and math might have been different for me.

"This woman had a Ph.D. in statistics. She was clearly over-qualified in terms of her level of education and yet under-qualified in her ability to teach me. It took until college to try to make up for what I missed, but once there, I had a wonderful teacher for Algebra. She could always come up with many different angles (no pun intended) to describe how it worked.

"Teaching an adult though is different. Unfortunately the bad experience sticks and I never really overcame my loss of confidence. I wanted to be an engineer, but the math-phobia kept me from it. Instead I majored in Sociology.

"I don't know what Mrs. Buck's deal was. I wish I had the brain then that I do now. I think it is only fair to expect that if she wants to teach eighth grade she should be able to think like an eighth grader."

David B.

Michael B., age 10
Pennsylvania, USA

Banned Words

"Doublespeak is a form of language that seems to communicate, but in reality does not."

William Lutz

Did you ever notice how almost everyone says "OK...so" just before talking about what needs to be done next, even when sometimes nothing really needs to be done. OK...so, many us have a few "bad habit" words that we use, especially for pausing. If you, umm, ever use them, they can make what you are saying ...umm... monotonous and boring, and then, like, the listener loses interest. So...words like the following should be banned from public speaking.

> Umm
> Alright
> So
> Everybody ready
> OK
> Then
> Well then, let's see

So, OK, you'll see how they get
used in the following story:

———————

"**D**id you ever have the teacher who never gets around to ever saying anything? These teachers have a whole vocabulary designed just for saying nothing – 'non-teach'ese I call it. They start off class by calling for everyone's attention. This is after having blown off the first five minutes of class. Then they ask, 'is everyone ready?' Then comes the 'um, ah, OK – … ready,' (pause) 'OK then, alright, – today we are going to, ah… you know. OK?'

"Then there's a little foot-pacing, as if now we really are getting ready. Then they begin again. It's as if they could 'teach' a whole class like this. 'OK then, um, maybe we can start by, well, ...' It makes you wonder what they really want to teach you. Some teachers have bigger 'non-teach' vocabulary than others. Watch out for them.

"I once had a teacher in a math class who only used 'um', but boy did he use it. In one class we counted them. He used 110 'ums' (long 'ums' at that) during class. You know the kind where you forget what came before the um. 'So, um... it is where the um... y-axis crosses, um..., the x-axis.' Then you ask yourself, 'What about the x-axis?' You don't remember what he was talking about, it was that long ago. It's not like he didn't teach anything but if he has to think that hard before saying anything, it makes you wonder. They should all be banned words.

"We did do some math though. After class we calculated that he used one 'um' on average every thirty seconds, and they took awhile. What does that leave for learning? It was driving me crazy and it affected class. This is one of those things that if you knew about it you probably wouldn't do it."

Dan H.

Paulina M., age 10
Santiago, Chili

Ditto That

"I figured I only had to take as many notes as there was free space on the hand outs."

Neil Goldstein

"Go easy on the dittos, don't bore us with the PowerPoints. I had an English teacher who every day would hand out at least five dittos that we would have to complete. We hate handouts.

"I would end up sleeping through class. It is really boring to try to learn something from handouts. She would teach from the handout or turn on the PowerPoint and stand there and just read off the PowerPoint. We could have done that on our own. The work was the most obvious thing and it didn't teach us anything that we could connect to the world.

"A lot of teachers just stand up and spew worthless info. A course taught by just reading the words is not set up to really teach. What I really want to be able to expect is that class is interesting, engaging, and challenges students. But it seems that most courses are targeted to just get everyone through. My friends and I always knew we could get by without even studying for the test. We would at least pass. In addition, what you needed to know to pass a test didn't mean jack in the real world. It's how you learn to apply the information you are given that makes a difference. I wish teachers knew how to make it relevant. I've had to learn most of what I know from the real world. The drill and fill, the dittos and Power-Points, they just don't cut it, they don't make class real."

Victor D., Age 11
Moscow, Russia

Mike W.

Class Struggle, More or Less?

Is getting homework a sign you have a good teacher?

_____

"Isn't the average amount of time a student spends on homework per week less than two hours and 15 minutes? If so, that means that our 'average student' is getting less than about half an hour of homework each school night, and as a result our 'average teacher' isn't having to correct very much either.

"Think of that student who has two hours of homework per night. Given the average then, there must be an awful lot of students who barely have to do any homework at all. I'm not here to judge if this is good or bad, but I do think that it distinguishes two types of teachers: the ones who give homework and those who don't. It has always seemed to me that the kids who didn't care about learning were always trying to get into the class with the teacher who didn't give homework. And the kids who were in the 'hard' courses always had a lot of homework. On the other hand, teachers have an immense challenge making homework useful and correctable with class sizes approaching 40 students per class.

"The teachers that I did the best with were the ones who gave thoughtful homework – not 'waste of time' homework – who cared how I did with it, held me accountable, and gave useful feedback. Somehow that made me feel more respected and helped me feel there was a standard that I had to keep. I know other students who have taken project-based classes where there isn't any homework. They often seemed so engaged and did lots of stuff outside of class around their project just because they wanted to (they didn't see it as homework).

"I think if you feel challenged and cared-for, you work better. I don't know the answer, but I do know that somehow it makes a difference to have a teacher who has real expectations of you."

Hannah E.

"Shakespeare" Man

"All the world's a stage, and all the people merely players. They have their exits and entrances; Each in their time plays many parts."

William Shakespeare

"When I was an undergraduate at the City College of New York, I chose as an elective a course entitled, 'Shakespeare's Time,' even though I understood the teacher was some kind of a twit. Believe me, beginning with the first session, our class found out that this instructor was as intolerant as they come. There was only one way to see it, his. I remember how some of us wanted to ask questions. The 'Shakespeare Man', as we called him, usually ignored our hands. And when he did acknowledge us, he didn't answer our question. His response was almost always, 'If you had only waited we would have gotten to that,' and without answering he would move on. One day he gave a woman student such a bad time, she ran out of the classroom, crying. He didn't seem to care. The thing is though he really knew his stuff and we were learning a lot.

"It presents a kind of paradox in teachers. I remember the morning he said to us, 'let me read you something from one of the plays.' When he finished, we all had puzzled looks on our faces. He noted wryly; 'Why aren't you laughing? I just told the funniest joke of the seventeenth century!' He helped us understand it and helped us enjoy it. With his breadth of knowledge and his 'feel' for the subject matter, he also gave us a great feeling for how spectators then stood around the play area and joked with the actors. You really had a sense of how it actually was in their time.

"So what is it you expect to get from a teacher? There is the human side – being treated with respect that makes the situation more conducive to learning. And then there's the content – the stuff you leave class knowing. Now, years later, I see that expectations in education are based on judgment calls. You can be lucky with one teacher and not so lucky with another. You can get good stuff in one way and difficult stuff in another all from the same teacher – a mixed bag."

Stan W.

It Isn't Fair

*"Teaching is not a lost art, but
the regard for it is a lost tradition."*
Jacques Barzun

"Did you ever have the teacher who doesn't teach you anything and doesn't give you enough work to be graded fairly? Well, that's my English teacher. We got our progress reports today. Usually I think most teachers are very fair in their grading and I respect them. After all, teaching hundreds of high school kids who don't seem to care, all day, must be tough.

"There is probably nothing else that makes you feel as alienated from your teacher and from your course more than being treated unfairly. It's not just about being graded unfairly, it is anything which keeps you from getting the most out of class. That's my English teacher. He doesn't seem to get that writing and homework are both part of English class. He doesn't assign any homework, for either reading or writing, and as a result we are not improving. We spent five weeks discussing *The Tempest*; that's all we did. Then we took the test. They were meaningless questions about what we did study, but also he tested us on material that had never even been covered.

"No one got above an 80 and, 'lo and behold,' our test grade was our ONLY grade for the quarter. He didn't assign any other work, or grade us on anything else, meaning that basically if you fail the test, you fail English. I got a C! I really try to work on my writing. I think I'm pretty good or at least would like the chance to be taught to be, and it's not happening. I have the right to expect to be given the opportunity to learn.

"I want to go into journalism, and if we did some writing and real learning then maybe, just maybe, I could get a decent grade in the class. I talked to him today and asked if we were ever going to do the things the other English classes have been doing (projects, writing, learning, etc.) and he said that we'll end up doing the same things they will, 'just differently.' This is what is so frustrating.

"It makes me wonder sometimes whether he really knows enough to teach. It is my expectation that if you want to be a teacher you should be prepared to teach, give assignments, spend the time to correct them, and help people see where they are headed in their learning. We can take it from there."

John K.

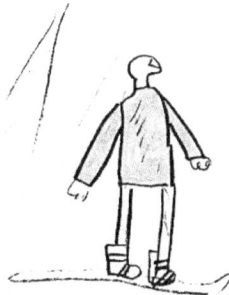

Trevor H., age 8
Colorado, USA

Tell 'Em What You're Gunna Tell 'Em

"Tell 'em what you're gunna tell 'em, tell 'em, then tell 'em what you told 'em."

Rules of the three part essay

In the previous story we asked is it fair to expect a teacher to cover enough material to teach you, and then to have sufficient assessments to measure your success? This story suggests that maybe we should be presented with the expectations of what we will gain ahead of time, and then be able to evaluate how successful it was, and we were, when we are done. Many States Department of Education now require that teachers give their classes a copy of the state standards. The goals should be indicated along with what the student should be able to expect to learn, and how they're going to get there. The idea of the three part essay fits right in.

"Yes, I have something to discuss. It is important to remember that there are some things that teachers teach that we hope will have a life-long impact. So my observation comes from having learned about the three-part essay. When I was in maybe middle school, I don't recall which grade, I remember distinctly that we were taught the rules or form of the three-part essay. Those rules seem to me to be what people should use whenever they are presenting, and teachers should use them, too.

"In order to write the essay, you needed an 'Introduction', a 'Main Topic' and a 'Conclusion'. In order to teach, a class should be structured the same way. Tell them what they are going to learn, teach them, and then review what you taught. The classes that I have been most successful in always had this clear process. The ones that I failed miserably in, didn't present the course in an organized way like this. The organization of the class and the quality of the presentation were critical to my success. I really respect things that are organized, and most of all, things that have a structure.

"I find it the same way when I am either a client or I am with clients. How well things are organized have an extreme impact on clarity and retention. It is very much the same with books, or the Internet, websites, or even walk- ing into a store. Ever noticed how easy things are to digest based after having an intro., then the presentation and finally the review?

"So this is what it comes down to: Tell them what you're going to be doing in the course. Be clear about the expectations and the results. Then go through the course just as you outlined it; then at the end review it and reinforce what has been taught. Don't do it just for the course but do it for each section. Do it for each day.

"I was convinced and still am, that this is the key to a well run class and the sign of a teacher who is prepared."

Henry T.

Anton M., Age 7
Berlin, Germany

Disorganized Teacher

As in the last story, a common complaint about teachers is about disorganization. Almost always it is because the teacher's organizational challenge has an impact on their learning or their grades. It may be funny to reflect upon it, though in some ways being disorganized is somewhat self-centered, and a real flaw. That does not honor the needs, and vulnerabilities of students. How can the teacher teach, or the student learn, in chaos.

"School presented some challenges, but in college I had a very disorganized English-Literature teacher. One semester, right before final grades were due, she sent emails to everyone in the class saying that she had lost her grade book and everyone should send her back, telling her what grades they had gotten on all their essays for the entire semester. It was really upsetting. It meant that there was no value to the work I had done. All the students were going to report whatever grades they felt like, and they would certainly be better than they really were, and she was going to use them to calculate their grades.

"Some students can learn for the love of it but most need the incentive and the structure of grades, real earned grades. Her lack of responsibility made my feelings towards her and of the course really change. I worked for this professor as a research assistant and later found out that she eventually, apparently, located the grade book. According to her it had fallen between her bed and the wall while she was grading papers late one night. I'm not sure I believed her and it made me wonder if she had kept any grades at all.

"She was very disorganized. During a different semester she gave me long lists of books that she wanted me to get from the library for her. One day

I made a list of the books that I couldn't find, and took it to the front desk. It seemed only natural to ask them to send out recall notices. (If a student has a book checked out and a professor wants it, the library sends out a recall notice and the student must return it.) The person behind the desk checked her computer, then went to consult with her supervisor. There followed a little conference. Finally the supervisor came over and said, 'I'm really not supposed to tell you the name of the person who has these items checked out, but …'

"It turned out that my professor already had all the books checked out. She probably lost them in the huge piles of stuff in her office and forgot that she had them. In some ways a story like this is humorous, but really it represents a condition that teachers should consider selfish"

Joan T.

NASA

A Better Match

"We are writing this because we found the teachers. We are parents of a high school student named Brad, who is currently attending an alternative public high school. Figuring out the best school and the best teachers for Brad has been difficult. But switching schools and having more committed teachers has made a huge difference. Those of you dealing with teachers who make it difficult for students know how we feel. We feel that these new teachers have much to do with Brad's motivation in being a better student.

"Before Brad started going to his new school, he attended the local public high school. It is a large school. Brad seemed to get lost in the crowd. He did not feel like he had a voice, and could not ask for help when he needed it. Mostly he felt ignored. There were too many students, and mostly the teachers seemed to be pushing the kids through the mill without really caring about them. There was no patience and no empathy. He felt confused and alone. It seemed to us that it's very easy for kids to go through schools like these and not actually learn anything of value.

"A critical observation to us about this new school is that the teachers all seem to want to be there, and they seem to love their jobs. Most of all, they respect the students and therefore the students respect the teachers. Brad is not lost in this school. He is recognized and has found his voice and is more actively engaged in learning. Since there is no homework given, he seems to put more effort into his work inside the classroom.

"Brad's last report card was his best ever for him in any school. This reward for hard work has done wonders for his confidence and self esteem. He now knows himself as a good student, capable of doing the things he wants to do. We now have expectations of how he will evolve as a person. Through his 'Careers' class he has begun an apprenticeship in wine making at a nearby vineyard and will have work after he graduates. Although Brad is not planning to go to traditional college like his older sister did, his new school has been just right for him and it has made it possible for him to graduate, which will be an accomplishment in itself. It did not seem like that would ever have been possible at the regular school.

"As his parents, we are both proud and happy that Brad has found a school where he feels important and engaged in learning, with teachers who care about him personally. He has new expectations of himself and of what is possible. It is an example of what a difference the teachers and their style of teaching can make in a kid's life and learning environment. We hope that we can encourage other students and parents to seek out positive solutions for themselves."

Rick and Marie L.

Emese H., age 9
Hungary

I Like It When...

"I like a teacher who gives you something to take home to think about besides homework."

Lily Tomlin as "Edith Ann"

I worked with a group of sixth graders and asked them to consider what it is about teachers and teaching that they like. What would they like to have as expectations from their teachers?

_____

"These are our expectations:

1) Finish one subject and don't just start another one, but let there be a little rest in between. It's hard to change pace and keep track.

2) Give homework that really helps, and don't give homework as a punishment just because the class didn't seem to work or understand that day.

3) Giving genuine support to the whole class makes us feel you really do believe in us and want us to do well.

4) Don't just impose authority, have it because you've earned it and deserve it. Don't just try to have authority and expect you'll be respected.

5) Give grades fairly, and don't give unfair grades for things that we can't control;
   a) never fail a kid who really tries
   b) give positive feedback for what we try hard at it.

6) Don't hold grudges. Let go of bad feelings when an issue is 'over and done with' and don't take it personally.

7) Stay focused on subjects in a fun way; tell stories that are fun to get into and relate to the subject matter; don't tell unrelated 'just talking because you can' stories.

8) Make real eye contact with the class and with each student. Don't just look above the class or not really at the class.

9) Know when to be serious and when to not be serious.
   a) don't get angry with the class after you have been joking around and you decide to get serious but we are still laughing.
   b) use sarcasm and humor carefully
      i) never use sarcasm in a way that will embarrass anyone. If it's about the subject matter, only use it when the class will understand it.
      ii) make sure that the jokes don't make the subject matter confusing. Sometimes after the joke we don't know what's true.

10) Don't take out anger or give punishment to the whole class when you are aware that 1 or 2 kids are responsible for the problem.

Anna., Age 7
Praha, Chech Rep.

Have-a-Heart

"Children seldom misquote you. In fact, they usually repeat word for word what you shouldn't have said."

Unknown

"Well, we had the principal. My son is very academic and doesn't do any sports. He is the quiet type and doesn't cause trouble. But he did not want to do athletics and he was being made to. Frustrated, he told the gym teacher that he didn't 'want to go to this school any more.' For this he was called into the main office with his father.

"My son's middle school principal told him his comment was not appreciated and 'in fact if something were to happen and you never returned again, no one would even notice.' Is this what we should expect from a principal? Imagine saying that to a young boy, in front of his father. I couldn't believe it and called the principal. You see my son took his words to mean that if he died no one would miss him.

"When I talked to the principal over the phone he became defensive and stated his comment was meant to 'motivate' my son to become involved in extra-curricular activities. He then went on a five minute-plus speech about a girl who died in a ski accident and because she was involved in many school related activities, she affected many lives and was very much missed.

"Nevertheless what he meant was that if my son died, no one would care. He went on with one of those condescending apologies, 'I'm sorry you feel the way you do.' I bit my tongue, instead of asking how long he had lived without a heart."

Connie M.

Where Were You?

"So when you are listening to somebody, completely, attentively, then you are listening not only to the words, but also to the feeling of what is being conveyed, to the whole of it, not part of it."

Jiddu Krishnamurti

After listening in on one of my meetings with a group of students, a teacher approached me to share how this letter, given to him by several of his students, changed him as a teacher. It influenced him in two ways. It had an immediate impact on how he taught. But perhaps more importantly, it showed him that what he thought of himself as a teacher was not the experience that the students were having. He felt that this letter helped him develop a sense of reflection on himself and empathy for his students. He had a better appreciation for their expectations of him and their hopes for themselves.

"Dear Mr. Driscoll,

"About these problems we have done lately; we feel that whenever me, Gustavo, or Jose have our hands raised in the air, you ignore us and not help us. It's frustrating when you spend all this time on the other side of the class. I know we can learn this but if you don't teach us we can't learn this.

"I know we have done this stuff for hella long now but I've tried to get help from you, but you said we have done this for too long now so tuff ... or that's what it seemed you were saying. I came after school and didn't get no help. I don't want to fail so I got a personal tutor to help me and Jose. I know I can pass this class because I have all A's and B's in my other classes. So this one I got to concentrate more in. So if you want to talk to us before or after school just let me know so I can make time. I'll tell my tutor to talk to you.

Sincerely,
Miguel M.
Jose E.
Gustavo M.

Did You Ever Have the inVisible Teacher

Chapter Six

"Any occurrence requiring undivided attention will be accompanied by a compelling need for distraction."

Robert Bloch

How to Get Your Teacher off Track?

One of my favorite kinds of class is when the kids come rushing into the classroom full of something that happened to them outside of class, and want to discuss it. In one such class, the buzz was about a basketball injury the night before. A student had unfortunately stepped on another player's head. They wanted to know about the forces involved, wanted to know the "physics." We figured how fast were they going when they hit the floor, we determined how much force and pressure was exerted. We also asked questions relating to the biology and reflected on how to feel about the situation. I would often tell a story of something that I knew that I thought was interesting and relevant. When class ended they left thinking "well we got him off track today," while I was checking off all the things in my class plan I had wanted to cover that day. They didn't even know what happened – or did they?...

At the beginning of the school year there are those few days spent getting the course up and running. I was explaining class rules, expectations, and going through the process of getting the textbooks distributed.

One kid in the back was looking at his textbook and raised his hand. "Mr. Russell, I think you ought'a see this." So I went back to his desk. He had his textbook open to the Table of Contents. There were twelve chapters, and four appendices, but in this particular book someone had added "Appendix E: Everything you need to know about Mr. Russell, page 287."

Turning to page 287 brought you to one of those pages left intentionally blank. On this page though, at the top, they had written "Appendix E: Everything you need to know to get Mr. Russell off track."

It listed eight items. Each was a different item designed to distract me and get me off track for the period. They were actually things I would talk about once in a while. Stories like about my wedding day (that ended in a horse buggy accident), or the story about building a car (a remake of an Austin Healey), but most importantly was "get him to talk about cosmology." They always thought that if they could get me going (as in "off track") by talking about the universe that would be worth a good chunk of time.

I thought that it was very funny. In fact I took the book to the teachers' room and copied the page on distraction techniques. Unfortunately, they regularly tried to use it.

I always thought that my using the stories that I told was a way of keeping their interest while supporting whatever I was teaching. After learning about "the appendix" I'm not so sure.

Hugo Y., age 6
Ontario, Canada

Mr. Tittle

*"The personal life deeply lived always
expands into truths beyond itself."*
                                    Anais Nin

Think of how invisible the janitor was
in "My teacher the Janitor," (p 30) or how
invisible "The Catholic Stutterer" (p 68)
would liked to have been. Here is a teacher
who helps students discover themselves, and
feel more visible to themselves and others.

———————

"My high school was Central High School in
Philly, (class #241). I had an English teacher named
Mr. Tittle. He was a 'tough as nails' grader and didn't
accept 'inadequate' work. He pushed us. He helped
me gain confidence in my writing skills and to become
more confident overall in my studies. I wrote a paper
on the book 'Great Expectations.' He worked with
me; didn't want me to fail. I got an A+ on it, and the
effect of that on me was incredible. My belief in
myself soared. He singled out my work as an
excellent paper and that 'it showed a very good way
to approach your work.' His doing that and not embar-
rassing me… well it was awesome. I was proud to
have my work seen by the others. He did this for all
of us whenever possible. I always think of Mr. Tittle
and his inspiration when I have a tough task to tackle
in work or life. Thanks Mr. Tittle."

Edward M.

Amazing Science Teacher

"Feed your brain and grow within."

Larissa B. – teacher

    When stories share how wonderful a teacher was, it seems they often refer to something more than just what they got from the subject, something beyond the curriculum. There is a real fondness and bond which develops between students and teachers when the student feels that they are being cared for, and prepared for life in some deeper way. Students seem to never forget that feeling. It influences how people see each other later on. No matter what they do in life, it helps mold the way they treat people when they are in a position to influence or lead.

———————

"Ninth grade, junior high school, I had an amazing science teacher, but one of the lessons I learned was more than just science. He had a great way of explaining things – like relating to his chronic allergies and the power of a sneeze. He explained to us how many miles per hour a sneeze could travel and told us that he actually threw his back out once by sneezing too hard!

    "Seventeen years later, there is one lesson that stands out in my mind. We were having a discussion on genetics in our Biology class. In our school there had been a major issue with racism and prejudice, just like most schools, and this teacher said he was fed up with it.

"He had two students, one black and one white, come to the front of the classroom and face the whole class. He said that sometimes in science we have to dig beyond the surface. Then he gave a graphic example: 'If you go beyond the skin from both of these guys what does it look like underneath?' He then used this as a way to go through and teach the systems, organs, etc.; all of them being the same in both people except the color of their skin. He not only taught us science but he helped us see each other in a different way.

"That day I learned to look beyond the surface of things. A good teacher pushes the limits, looks for new ways to convey information, stimulate learning, and finds real life examples that lead a student to use the information throughout life. He gave real meaning to what we did in class."

Nichole R.

Andreas N., Age 10
Kungsor, Sweden

A Separate Piece

"In no school that I saw anywhere in the United States were non-white children truly intermingled with white children. ... The duel society, at least in public education, seems in general to be unquestioned."

Jonathan Kozol

———————

"This is not a story about a teacher I had, as I am a teacher myself. It's about a student I had who shared a story with me about her biology teacher. To the outsider our school appeared to be very diverse. In fact though, there was little interaction between the various ethnic groups and different races. We were approximately one-quarter Hispanic, Asian, White, and African-American. At lunch you noticed that everyone would divide up into their groups, and then primarily stayed separated. Even though the community prided itself on diversity, within the school the students remained segregated by their own choice. We did not have tracked programs that divided students. Everyone was free to take whatever class they wanted, if they could get in, Somehow, though, the classes ended up ethnically separated. What were the forces at play here?

In my classes for example, I had no mixed groups. For whatever reason, my advanced class, the college prep class, was all white and Asian, while the other regular class was all Hispanic and African-American. I had many good students in each of my classes. Why weren't more students trying to be in the more advanced classes? I asked them and here is the story I got from one African-American girl:

"I really wanted to be part of the college prep program. I was excited about it and thought I could do well. I signed up for College Prep Biology, but the teacher never gave me a chance. She never let up on me for being the one different student.

"I attended every class, did all the work and was a more committed student than many others. I worked really hard but it wasn't easy. One day she gave us a homework assignment about DNA and how it is identified. It was completely new material and she had assigned it without even having introduced it to us yet. I tried to do the assignment but I couldn't. The next day, while in front of the class, she saw that I didn't have my homework. She asked me why. I explained to her what had happened and asked her for help. Instead of recognizing that she should have prepared us to do the work, she pointed out that I was the only black student in the class and added, 'You'll have to do better than that young lady – you're lucky you're in here at all.' I was embarrassed, mortified, and, even though what she said wasn't fair, I felt ashamed. I wished I were invisible. I dropped out of that course and came back to the 'regular' bio class, because it was the only place I could feel comfortable or feel like I belonged."

"At this point she was crying and the rest of our class made it clear they understood it also."

Norman R.

Collaborate

Sometimes teachers make students feel like they just don't matter. One way teachers do this is by failing to give students a chance to talk with them, to work out problems or get help from them. They are out of the building as soon as class or the school day is over, and they don't provide any other access. I had a student tell me that when she went to her teacher for help he said, "I explained that in class, I'm not going to waste my time doing it again." Little wonder some students end up feeling helpless and unsupported. Proper use of teacher authority, encouragement, support, and feedback, make a difference in student educational success.

———————

"On exam day I was sick. I couldn't make it; I was at the doctor's office. I emailed my Instructor and TA that I could not make it and needed to make arrangements for a retake. He did not respond. The TA said the Instructor had the final say and suggested that I keep trying to reach him. I wrote again and included my original message just in case it was overlooked. I kept writing for four weeks, with no response. I went to his office - never there. Where was this guy? Outside of class he was invisible. Finally, my TA told me that even though the Instructor had gotten my emails, my grade was a zero.

"I was really angry. My teacher was having a negative effect on my education. He failed me as a teacher, and as a professional. My TA was the only one who tried to help. So I wrote the teacher one last email telling him how disappointed I was with how he handled this situation, and offered my opinion of him as an educator. He responded to that one.

"I'm not the only one. Lots of us have to deal with this. What does this mean for you? Let's stop simply complaining and do something about teachers who fail to communicate, or who are simply unprofessional. We complain to each other instead of to the teachers. Perhaps we are afraid they will change our grades because we complain.

"To get results, we need to go directly to the problem, but we become unnerved. Why? Because if we piss the teacher off he can manipulate our grade and we'll do even worse. It isn't fair having our grades based on how we make the professor feel. Since when does it say on the syllabus: 'Relationship with instructor – 50% of final grade?' A grade should be based on the quality of the work done and a student should not be prevented from demonstrating that.

"There are basic expectations for students, and there must also be the same for teachers. I accepted the responsibility to get my assignments made up. They should cooperate with us when we try, and not penalize us for things we cannot control. Teachers must make sure that we are given real ways to communicate with them and then follow through and see that it works.

"Teachers who are responsible and good at their job deserve a big 'thank you!' You'll never know how much we appreciate you. But let's stand up for ourselves when it comes to our rights in the classroom. The 'end-of-semester anonymous evaluation' will not solve the problem. The problem-teacher doesn't read them anyway. If you are not satisfied with your instruction, you have to let the instructor know, and then the administration. I did. By the end of the semester the school had worked with him to communicate better and I was allowed to take my test."

Dave J.

A Place to Hide

"What lies ahead of us and what lies behind us are tiny matters compared to what lies within us."

Ralph Waldo Emerson

"**W**ell yes, I had the teacher; in fact I've known many teachers. I am the superintendent of a small school district in the Midwest. I know that perhaps this is a little unusual in terms of stories about teachers, but I think this story represents an important issue; one that affects what students end up remembering and of their feeling about their teachers.

"A teacher of mine at our high school, characterized a poorly recognized but serious problem. She gradually started spending more time in her classroom and rarely came out of her room. She became known to the students as the teacher who gave out candy during break, but was always forgetting things like attendance or missing "Open House" night at school. I call this the 'self-isolated teacher,' perhaps you've had one.

"One of the great things about teaching, and one of the problems as well, is that teachers have their own space, their own little universe in which to educate; it is their classroom. It is here they have the opportunity to make wonderful things happen, where they can use their creativity and personalities to help kids to develop, personally and educationally.

Michael S., age 6
Pennsylvania, USA

"But when, for a variety of reasons, a teacher starts to feel alienated; they tend to come out of their classroom less and less. If a teacher is having problems getting grades in on time or fulfilling other administrative or social commitments, they tend to avoid their peers. To other teachers, the isolated teacher begins to be invisible.

"Sometimes the problem might be because they're relating more to students than to their professional peers; other times they have no relationship with students and other teachers realize that. The problem, for the isolated teacher, is that they may have a failing relationship with the administration, a vulnerability to other teachers or, perhaps, too strong a connection with students. As a result they have a diminishing sense of belonging to the school. The process tends to feed on itself.

"The isolated teacher ends up teaching less effectively and becomes more alienated from the school. It has been my experience that by the time the problem becomes clear, it is already serious and often too late. Then how do you reach them?

"Teachers are central to us. They are important to the student, the parents, teachers and administrators, and to the community. Offer to help and let them know. If the teacher could see it, they might be able to get help for what is driving them away"

Charles E.

Two Teachers

"One looks back with appreciation to the brilliant teachers, but with gratitude to those who touched our human feelings. The curriculum is so much necessary raw material, but warmth is the vital element for the growing plant and for the soul of the child."

Carl Jung

This chapter is about visibility. The last two stories were about teachers who make themselves invisible. A situation that is perhaps more important is the student who wishes to be invisible. It might be hard to remember, but when you were in that classroom, you were given very little personal empowerment. The teacher set the environment and determined what you are (and aren't) allowed to do. The only way to exert your own control was to "act-out," for which you got in trouble, or just become invisible, and hope that it will all pass. You know, like the student who sits in the back and reads. In this story, unlike our last story about collaboration, this young student finds someone who reaches her, appreciates her, encourages her to excel, and helps her want to be visible.

———————

"Did you ever have the teacher? Well I did, Miss Durland, first grade. It's hard to believe but I flunked the first half along with six others. Miss Durland used adhesive to seal the mouths of the orally wayward. A friend of mine and I regularly qualified. I also had the distinction of assignment to the dunce stool with the appropriate hat to be worn when sitting there.

"She was a slight middle-aged woman who wore smocks buttoned at the wrist and neck. Her hair was always 'just so.' Her pursed lips were so tight you might have had to use a crow bar to get her to smile. You could tell just saying a nice 'good morning' was a chore. When she was in the room I would try to remain unnoticed, but I imitated her for the benefit of my fellow victims whenever she left.

"I was at my wits end and felt very badly about myself. A teacher friend of my father, Miss Durkee, began to tutor me. I'd go to her house three times a week and we'd sit at the dining room table with the fragrant lilac bush just outside the window. It wasn't so much what she taught, because she taught everything, but she was always so delighted with me. She never got over telling me how well I was doing. Reward at the end of my lessons was a Hershey with almonds, to this day my favorite candy. She took me to the creamery to see how butter and cream were processed. She reserved tickets to the ballets that came to Omaha because I loved dance and took ballet lessons. She never forgot my birthday, even long after our lessons were over. From then on, no matter what, I stood out in my classes and was successful.

"I think without someone like Miss Durkee to have helped me enjoy learning, the experience of Miss Durland might have been a bad legacy instead of a humorous memory."

Barbara T.

Vanja B., Age 7
Minnesota, USA

Stay out of Ice Cream Shops

"The true Republic: men, their rights and nothing
more; women, their rights and nothing less."
Susan B. Anthony

More than one hundred years ago Ellen
Hyde, principal of the Framingham Normal
School, wrote: "To hear lessons and control
restless children six hours a day through thirty-
six weeks in the year is wretched drudgery, but
to train and develop human minds and characters
is the most inspiring work in the world."

Ellen E., Age 3
North Dakota, USA

"Among the hurdles that female
teachers had to overcome was the
right to keep their jobs when they
married. In Massachusetts, teacher
Mary Murphy was fired for misconduct as a result of marrying in
1901. She took the case to court. The
judge ruled in her favor, pointing out
the obvious that 'marriage was not
misconduct' and was not, therefore,
grounds for her dismissal from her job."

However, the restrictions on
women teachers persisted. Here is
a list of those contractual restrictions:

Rules of conduct For Teachers anno 1915

1. You will not marry during the term of your contract.

2. You are not to keep company with men.

3. You must be home between the hours of 8 p.m. and 6 a.m. unless attending a school function.

4. You may not loiter downtown in ice cream shops.

5. You may not travel beyond the city limits unless you have the permission of the chairman of the board.

6. You may not ride in a carriage or automobile with any man unless he is your father or brother.

7. You may not smoke cigarettes.

8. You may not dress in bright colors.

9. You may under no circumstances dye your hair.

10. You must wear at least two petticoats.

11. Your dresses must not be any shorter than two inches above the ankle.

12. To keep the school room neat and clean, you must: sweep the floor at least once daily, scrub the floor at least once a week with hot, soapy water, clean the blackboards at least once a day, and start the fire at 7 a.m. so the room will be warm by 8 a.m.

A Piece of Ice

'The reason I always try to meet and know the parents better is because it helps me to forgive their children."

Louis Johannot

This story is from a woman who spent her whole career as a school secretary. As well as believing that she was as much a "teacher" as a secretary, she was also a mandated reporter. She had a special role in seeing the invisible child. It is about a girl whose whole world changed when she became "visible."

———————

"As school secretary I found myself involved in kids' lives in every possible way. I, as it is with teachers, am mandated to report when a situation arises which might indicate signs of abuse. I question sometimes what service we provide when the system takes over and children's lives are changed forever. This is an experience I had..."

"It's 'pencil time.' Kids lined up at recess to buy the swirling designs and colors for a quarter. But outdoor play also brings the inevitable flow of 'sick 'n injured,' competing with the phones, would be registrants, delivery and work persons, waiting parents and frantic teachers, in a loud and chaotic ballet of sound and fury. I am facing three stomach aches in a row.
      'What is this! Did you eat it?'
      'No.'
"It was a constant flow of kids. 'No wonder your stomach hurts. I'm sending you to the Outreach Room for food. Whose next?' The tall, slight fifth grader with the scrap of paper nods. 'Is this your note? Your head hurts?' 'Is it a headache, or did something hit it?'
      'My father hit me.'

"My stomach churns. She tells me more; her father struck her yesterday, 'near the ear.' But she is holding her forehead. I thought about bringing her into the empty principal's office and giving her ice. It wouldn't help. She looked so tired. It wasn't the first time. I could see that. She was visible now.

"Now the swirling was all on the outside as we entered Act Two. It wasn't just her and me now. There were new characters: the principal, Child Protective Services, the police and new foster parents. Imagine in the space of two hours being assigned a substitute mother and father. Imagine going to school in the morning from one home and returning to a new street, area, and family after school.

"Three o'clock - I can't let it go. I am like a bird with wings soaked in oil, dirt and heavy grease. What is it like to hit a child again and again? What is it like to be hit?

"There are new parents, but where did the child go?"

Charlotte S.

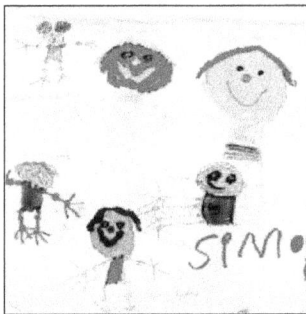

Simone D., Age 4
Massachusetts, USA

A Letter to My Teacher

I asked a group of recent high school graduates to put together "the letter" they would like to send their teacher, if they could, offering some helpful thoughts. In it they would express what would make a difference to them to help learning be more successful. After discussing it, going online, and putting their thoughts together, this is the letter they wished to send. This is the third of the four lists for teachers in the book, (*Teachers of the Craft* p 36, *I like it When* p 116, and the upcoming story about third graders on p 178). The similarities kind of sum it up. Notice they have as much to do with how they wish to be treated as they do with how they want to be taught.

"Dear Teacher,

1. Let me be me: Let me work on problems in the way that works best for me and adjust your style to help bring me along.

2. Be forgiving: Let me ask questions and help me answer them, and if I get it wrong, let me do it over again, helping me break the problem into its parts. It would help to give me useful hints instead of just letting me feel stupid.

3. Don't intimidate: If I didn't understand what you just said or did, don't just repeat it. If I'm confused, repeating it will only intimidate me and confuse me more. When you include a lot of unrelated material it scares me and I can't think. Don't make tests look scary and don't make the questions so different from the material we studied that we can't understand them.

4. My mind shuts down: Don't put a time limit on answering questions, it just makes me panic and I can't think.

5. Please be patient with me: I'm really trying to understand – so if I don't get it the first way you present it, try it a different way, but don't abandon me.

6. Please help me be comfortable in not knowing, because I won't know it until I've finished not knowing it. Let me struggle through not knowing it and give me positive feedback when I finally do.

7. Be nice, have compassion: Even when I really understand the material, I can still get all the test questions wrong. So help me show you what I understand through whatever way works for me.

8. Don't go too fast: When presenting new material, give me time to write down each step, and don't go on or assign homework until you know I understand it.

9. Prepare us: Please never assign homework before we have been taught it. I get so frustrated when sometimes you assign me homework before I understand it.

10. Let me learn: Don't forget that I want to learn and retain it. But realize that some subjects are harder for some students than others and that can be traumatic. The moment that I start to think that I can't learn this, I get overwhelmed. Sometimes I feel panic. Be understanding that I try and sometimes I fail and that's OK because I will keep trying until I get it. Please help me do that. These can be emotional subjects. Pity will not help me at all, but support, positive feedback, patience and individual attention will.

Sincerely,
Your Favorite Student

Against The Odds

"To understand the world, one must not be worrying about one's self."

Albert Einstein

"This story really belongs more to Mr. Roule than it does to us, I think, because he was up against some great odds to teach us, let alone to become a favorite teacher. You see, my high school was 75% Jewish (at least) and 25% (other whites). That was as diverse as it got. Mr. Roule was black.

"I still don't know how he did it – to make himself a part of our lives and to make us see him as a role model. Oh, I understand how the kids got friendly with him and learned to trust him – he was very involved with sports (assisted), and he came to all our functions. He was different than the other teachers. He actually seemed like he was really enjoying himself instead of 'being a teacher.' He was also young, probably just out of college. All of that is a partial explanation. There was something special about him. After all, he taught Biology. To say it wasn't my favorite subject would understate the obvious.

"Somehow or other he made learning Biology fun. It was the way he made you feel when in his class. In some classes you just wanted to hide, that's the best way to get by, but not in Mr. Roule's class. You were not intimidated or afraid; you wanted to be there."

Mitchell G.

Birthday Wish

"It's a very, very Mad World.
Children waiting for the day they feel good.
Happy Birthday, Happy Birthday.
Made to feel the way that every child should.
Sit and listen, sit and listen.
Went to school and I was very nervous,
no one knew me, no one knew me.
Hello teacher tell me what's my lesson.
Look right through me, look right through me."

Michael C., age 11
N. Carolina, USA

From "Mad World" by Gary Jules

Did You Ever Have the Teacher

Trust

Chapter Seven

"Words have the power to both destroy and heal. When words are both true and kind, they can change our world."

Buddha

Endocarditis

One day we were talking about disease processes, and entered into the area of autoimmune diseases. It's an interesting topic. An illness stimulates the immune system, that then attacks the invaders and we're all better. Well, most of the time. Sometimes after the infection, the body goes on attacking its own cells that were involved in the infection and ends up destroying them. This possibly includes diseases like some diabetes and perhaps even multiple sclerosis. We began to discuss how strep throat can be a very dangerous illness if not treated because it can go on to become scarlet fever and rheumatic fever, and ultimately end up causing an inflammation of the heart. This last condition is known as endocarditis, an auto-immune disease in which the body starts attacking the heart. "It can be difficult to treat," I said, "and you can die from it,"

All of a sudden this girl gasps. "Mr Russell, I have endocarditis, am I going to die; am I dying?" It's so easy to think that you are presenting the class with something you think they might find fascinating without stopping to realize what the consequences of it might be. Certainly not everybody with endocarditis dies. She started crying and was very upset. I felt like I had broken an unspoken trust as I stood there trying to figure out how to comfort her, realizing that part of the trust is to ask a few questions and be careful what you say.

In Teacher We Trust

*"No soul is desolate as long as there is a human
being for whom it can feel trust and reverence."*
T. S. Eliot

———————————

"My teacher story is about the love and
dedication of one of my elementary school teachers
and how profoundly she affected my entire life for the
better. Her name was Aline Bateman, and she was my
fourth grade teacher. She was a young, pretty teacher,
with whom I immediately fell in love.

"I didn't realize it at the time, but it was just her
second year of teaching, and she had been assigned to
perhaps the worst school in the city. It was the worst
because of the area in which it was situated, and the
problems associated with a very poor neighborhood.

"That was my neighborhood. There were many
days I went to school without breakfast and went
home to a meager lunch, but I was as happy as a kid
could be under the circumstances. At the beginning of
the year I was unable to pay my book rental fee, and it
was coming down to the deadline. Although I didn't
know it, Aline paid them for me. This would be the
first of many times she would help me, not only with
money but with real emotional propping up.

"The academic side of grade school was never a
problem for me, but there were, of course, always the
problems of the neighborhood that intertwined with
attending school. I did my best to avoid confrontation
with the school bullies, but there were times when it
was impossible. It was after one of these confronta-
tions that Aline first helped me avoid real trouble.

"I was carrying newspapers before school each
morning. I gave most of what I earned to my mother,

but I did save a small amount each week for what had been a dream for me.

"I wanted to buy a navy 'P' coat. I barely had enough money to buy it, but I finally did. One of the bullies didn't think I should have such a nice coat. I heard a noise behind me and turned around. He was urinating on the back of my new coat. He laughed and said, 'Well, it's a 'pee' coat, ain't it?'

"I flew into a rage I had never before experienced. I jumped on him, smashing his face into the street over and over. The fact that he was a bully and had beaten up on so many kids didn't make any difference to our principal. He was getting so much heat from the parents that he was considering expelling me from school. That's when Aline came to my rescue in a big way. She argued with the principal that I was well within my rights to defend myself. She finally won out, and I loved her even more than before.

"She continued to buy pencils, paper and pay my book rental as I progressed on through the next four grades. At the time I thought Aline was doing all this for me alone. I found out later she did it for many of the children at our school.

"During the last five years of grade school my mother was being treated for cancer. My father, who was trying to earn a living for his children, finally gave up and left my mother to finish raising seven of her children on her own. It was a traumatic experience to suddenly be without a father, but thanks to the love of my mother, we managed to handle not only the economic side of his leaving, but also the emotions associated with it. Things really got tough though, and two of my older sisters had to go to work to help us survive. We were also receiving aid from the state and many good neighbors.

"Then, in April, just before my graduation from the eighth grade, tragedy struck. My mother finally succumbed to the cancer that had been slowly killing her. We kids were all devastated. I took my mother's death as hard as anyone could ever take a loved one's death. I immediately began to get in trouble every day at school and went out of my way to cause myself problems. I was angry at the world and what it had done to me, and I was wallowing in self-pity and hurt. I had lost my trust in everything. This resulted in my being called into the principal's office several times a week. I still did my schoolwork, but otherwise I was a real menace.

"I don't know what I had done to be called to the principal's that day, but on my way, Aline stopped me. She had been to see the principal, and led me to the small teachers' lounge in the basement to talk to me. It was all one sided, but this pretty, brown haired, blue eyed, petite lady changed my life.

"'Bill, I know life has been very unfair and you've had things really hard all your life, and you have every right to be mad at the world. You have every right to get into the trouble you've been getting into. I won't tell you not to be mean, but I also want to tell you, you have the ability to rise above all that. You're too bright to let all of this ruin your life. I know your mother would want you to make something of yourself, to do something with your life. You need to show everyone how good you are. You need to show them you're stronger than revenge against the world for all it's done to you.

"'You don't have to live in this neighborhood or be poor your whole life and I know you'll do something worthwhile with yourself. Do you know how disappointed I'd be if you didn't?" She took my hand in hers and said, 'Bill, I truly care about what happens to you. I'll always support you and be your friend. I'll always be here for you to talk to. I talked to your mother a while back, and she, too, said she had great hopes for you to do something with your life. You may not know how much she wanted you to get out of this neighborhood and do well. I beg you to please do what's right even though you have every right to be angry. It will not only make me very proud, but you'll be able to be very proud of yourself. You have to rise above all this and accept what you can be. Accept what you are destined to be. Trust in yourself and in God.'

"I remember this conversation and I realize how much a teacher can influence. I did change after that. No one had ever told me I could get out of that neighborhood or not be poor the rest of my life. I think I changed after that because I respected and trusted Aline very much. I didn't want to disappoint her.

"Many times since then I've thought about Aline and how much she influenced me. There have been times when I have asked myself, 'would Aline approve of this?' If she gave me nothing else, she gave me a positive attitude about my abilities and myself. I eventually became an officer in the United States Army and found myself in dire straits many times. These were the times I relied on God and the wisdom of Aline to see me through... and it worked.

"I have absolutely no doubt that she saved my life. It's hard to say what direction my life might have taken without her consul, but I know it would not have been good. The teacher who can build trust, inspire students to learn and become somebody, deserves to be called 'Hero,' right along with Aline Bateman, because they too, will save lives."

Bill M.

Pregnant at 16

"The present is saturated with the
past and pregnant with the future."
Gottfried Wilhelm Leibniz

Whether we like it or not, much of the social support that young people get comes through the school system. Personal responsibility, citizenship skills, personal hygiene, and understanding values have all partly become the domain of the classroom and school. In addition, teachers have always been a major source of advice, of guidance, and of a safe place, in which students place a great deal of trust. We all remember the teacher who spent the time to help us, or someone we knew, through a hard phase. Most students have had a teacher that they could go to when they needed a little help. Imagine being pregnant in high school. It must be filled with the difficulty of acknowledging what is real and of wanting it to be different, of needing affirmation for the positive, and support in the midst of sadness. It must be confusing to receive confirmation from some and disapproval by others. One would hope that it is the teacher who would give what is needed to help make a deliberate choice to move on.

———————

"When I was a junior in high school, I discovered I was pregnant. It was a moment of profound confusion. My life was really disrupted. Many girls who wound up pregnant at 16 had an abortion but I knew from the beginning I was going to keep my baby. At a moment like that I wanted to be able to trust in someone. I wanted to turn to those adults around me and be helped to go from a sense of dread to at least an unsure sense of excitement about what lay ahead for me. I knew that life was going to be very different. What I'm getting at is that I had that teacher who knocked me down at the very moment that I needed a boost, some guidance on how to handle this successfully. He violated the trust I had in him.

"He called me a failure and actually said that now I would amount to nothing. 'You're just another statistic' and then he said I was a joke and he laughed right into my face. I stood there 5 1/2 months pregnant, and the way he had made me feel was that I wished I were dead. I remember holding back the tears just long enough so that I could leave the room. I didn't want him to get the satisfaction out of seeing the tears roll down my face.

"There was no stopping what was going to happen. I was going to have a baby. It just seems cruel that he would want me to feel so worthless. As the end of the pregnancy approached, I left school. I wound up giving birth to a beautiful baby boy and was home tutored for the remainder of the year. Then the next year I came back to school to finish with my senior class. I still had that same teacher. He didn't let up. He would shake his head as I walked past, saying things under his breath.

"I couldn't take it so I dropped out, got my GED instead, and went to college. I am very satisfied with my life now, although his negative behavior limited my choices and changed the course of my life. But yes I had a teacher who never should have been allowed to become a teacher in the first place. He should never been allowed in the classroom, a place which should be there to help young people become full people. A place which should be filled with trust.

"A teacher wants to be unforgettable in students' minds, because of what they did for the better. Boy didn't he wind up being unforgettable for all the wrong reasons."

Barbara B.

Shepherds and Teachers

'Trust is not a given. It has to be earned. And in an interdependent relationship as the one teachers have with students, without trust there is often only a stagnant environment... Whether adults or children, we don't learn if we don't trust."

Rebecca Alber

"Once I estimated that between the start of my sophomore year and the end of my senior year, I had written a total of maybe 250 dreadful poems. My 'MO' was to bring them to my English Professor, Robert Cording, late at night and slip them under his office door. These were real abominations, but he never tried to duck me. He had endless patience, and he could see that, while there wasn't much promise in my work, there was a kind of crucial need behind my scribbling.

"And so, he talked to me. He gave me guidance. And as time went by he even gave me a typewritten copy of his own first manuscript that I still treasure. He commented, in that tiny handwriting that still sends chills through his students, on every one of my terrible student poems. Until, in my senior year, as we sat hunched over a poem of mine, he said to me, 'I think you should be writing fiction.'

"Perhaps he had finally reached the end of his patience. Or maybe that poem was simply so bad that he wanted to save poetry from me. Either way, the comment backfired. I kept at it.

"I credit him with helping me publish my first short story, with teaching me to write a query letter, and of telling me, on a Cape Cod beach, as we watched our wives walk ahead of us, to be careful that my life not become fodder for my work. But most of all, I think, I credit Bob with teaching me how to 'read.'

"It was a moment. I was sitting in his poetry class, and we were working over Elizabeth Bishop's poem, "Sandpiper." And, as he asked those questions designed to make us participants in explication – something happened to me. Even now, the best explanation I can provide is that, in a moment of trust, epiphany and grace, the poem ceased being an academic exercise. It suddenly had a critical relationship to my life. Bishop's vision became my vision, and I understood things I had not previously understood. It is not hyperbole to say this was a moment of conversion. I left that classroom light-headed. I had the feeling of becoming a different person.

"I have had many conversations with others about teachers that ended with something like 'John Wilson was my shepherd,' or 'Tom Lawler really turned me around,' or 'Clyde Pax cared about what happened to me.' I encourage anyone to send your tribute to your own particular mentor, the teacher whom you trusted and changed your life."

Jack O.

Joseph T., Age 9
Virginia, USA

151

Bad Grader

*"You know how Einstein got bad grades
as a kid? Well, mine are even worse!"*

Calvin and Hobbes

———————

"Grades are supposed to be an objective measure of a student's performance in class, no more, no less. We should have faith in our grade. People say grades are only letters and numbers. They can't represent our inner talents, ambitions, skills and individuality. Even worse, sometimes we get graded on things that have nothing to do with the work we put into the class. If there is one thing that we should expect from a teacher is that the grade is fair, not just to one student, but to all of them. We trust that a teacher will understand that each student's work is different and grade them fairly.

"I was fortunate enough to take classes that people older than I would take. For the most part, teachers supported me. I was simply another student.

"However, Ms. Goran, my honors mathematics teacher, right from the start, gave me a hard time about my age. At the beginning of the semester, she openly questioned my ability to compete with the older students. In front of the class she declared 'no sophomore can succeed in my class' (the class was usually only for juniors).

"I felt terrible and singled out. In the beginning I struggled and barely passed the first few tests. It wasn't just me though, many other students were struggling.

"Ms. Goran gave us a handout describing her grading policy. She weighed the second semester more heavily than the first, allowing for room to improve, and I really improved. By the end of the course, I showed I was able to handle the class, obtaining a 'B' average under her grading system. Much to my dismay, Ms. Goran decided to change her grading policy, with no explanation, by weighing each semester's grade equally. It resulted in a 'C' for me instead. I couldn't believe it. It was stated right there in her grading policy. It made me feel as if she did it to give me the lowest grade possible. I trusted her and tried my hardest by her rules, and she didn't live up to it.

"It wasn't fair. In order to be treated fairly, I had to argue for it. Only after a lengthy fight, did I get the grade any other student who improved the way I did, deserved. I felt I was given a grade before the semester even started. It seemed like knowing that I was 'different' increased the pressure I had in the class. When I attended lectures, turned in homework and took tests, I imagined in the back of my mind, Ms. Goran taking extra care to take points off of my work.

"She made me feel like I was graded before I started. Every minute in her class was intimidating and alien-ating. That I couldn't trust her made me feel like an outsider and not good enough to be taught by her.

Jennifer Y.

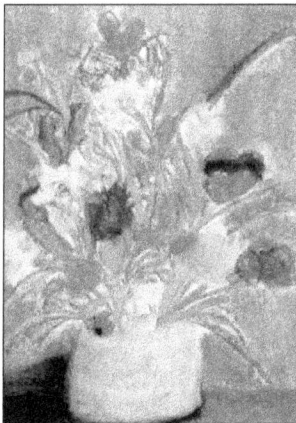

Michael B., Age 10
Pennsylvania, USA

Under God

*"Patterning your life around other's
opinions is nothing more than slavery."*

Lawana Blackwell

In many courses there is often a fine line between giving
students enough information to make an informed opinion and
pushing them to accept your own thoughts on the subject. It is
especially important that one does not hold them accountable for
accepting those views. I found this problem, for example, when
teaching about nuclear energy. How do you inform them about
the scientific and political issues without imbuing the subject
with your own conclusions? If a student is not free to form their
own informed opinions then they may be deprived of becoming
independent thinkers. It takes trust to present one's own ideas to
a teacher and believe that they will help develop those thoughts,
and not be required to accept theirs. If they don't trust that their
teacher will help them develop independent thoughts, they are at
risk of feeling alienated and not free to further explore their own
thinking or to speak up in the future.

————————

"I loved my fourth grade teacher. She was clever and
interesting and very upbeat. She made coming to school
every day feel exciting. I felt like she enjoyed being with us
too. I even had decided that year to become a fourth grade
teacher when I grew up. That's why when the following
happened I felt so confused and distraught, and why I lost
my trust in her.

"I grew up in a pretty conservative middle class community.
My parents were humanists and atheists and like most nine
year olds, how they thought about most things influenced
how I did too. I was aware that we were a bit 'different.'
But I felt proud of my family and accepted among my peers.
At school though, when each morning we recited the 'Pledge
of Allegiance,' I very quietly left out the words 'under God.'

"One day my revered fourth grade teacher told us about atheists and explained how we must feel sorry for these people because they don't 'believe' and that we should even pray for their salvation. I went home very upset never having imagined that something that my family and I believed, might be shameful, and that someone else considered it sinful to have such thoughts. I was especially upset that it was my teacher who was saying it; someone I trusted and believed knew the truth. Even in this confusion though, my allegiance was definitely with my parents. I resented that I had to think about choosing sides. My teacher had no idea the impact her words had on me. She alienated me and made me feel less a part of her class. I'm sure she just thought she was imparting a lesson on forgiveness and tolerance, and of righteousness.

"Instead of becoming a fourth grade teacher I became a therapist, helping people figure out for themselves what they believe."

Martha L.

Amand C., age 9
Tennessee, USA

FINAL EXAMINATION

Do not begin until you are told to do so!

**You are required to use a number 2 pencil.
If you do not, your test will be void and
you will _fail_ this examination!**

1) Why do teachers make tests seem so intimidating?

a) because they enjoy making students feel stupid
b) because it makes the teacher feel so much smarter
c) they believe that it challenges students to really think

   ○ a
   ○ b
   ○ a and b
   ○ b and c
   ○ all of the above

Still kind of gets you, doesn't it?

_____

Many people experience intense anxiety when being assessed. Is this how we want people to feel when taking a test? So why do we make the assessment as intimidating as possible? What is it we're measuring? A student once said to me, "Why wouldn't a teacher make it so we feel trusted and comfortable and excited to show what we know? It shouldn't be like a contest to see how many students can be knocked off the grading ladder." Most of us would like to show what we know, and to do so in a trusted and supported way.

"Remember 'The Paper Chase?' A couple of students are so panic stricken that they have to escape from campus in order to be able to study for their final exam. One of them exclaims 'panic has descended.' They end up checking into a motel. They then have the management remove anything from the room that might distract them because their state of fear was so high. Fear was the driving force, not the love of learning, or the desire to show (with pride) what they had learned.

"I had a teacher, Miss Bentley. When we had a test she would make us sit with our backs to each other in alternating seats. If you even looked towards another table she would grab your paper and give you a zero. She would walk around and act like a prison guard, like maybe we might escape.

"The question remains. Why is there a need to perpetuate this environment of intimidation when it comes to assessment. We all went through it. Did it somehow make us better learners? Did it somehow make us stronger for the challenges ahead, like having faced up to the bully in the school yard. Is that it, so we are now stronger and won't get bullied in the future? If we all went through it, is it really what we want now to be doing it to others? Think of making your environment at home like that, or your place of worship. It would be awful. I can't imagine my life that way, so why do we keep doing it to others? I have a friend who, when asked to recite the ten commandments, does so with fear because of what he went through to learn it. Interestingly, he never goes to church now.

"I don't want that kind of stress in my life and I don't want to put others through it, so in my work, when teaching other employees new information, I ask them to trust me, and I try to make it fun. I try to invite them to be proud of showing what they can do as a result of their new knowledge, not scared.

"Is this how you want to be treated? Let's see ourselves differently, and as a result make a difference in others' lives."

Gordon S.

Children of Greenhorns

'This train don't carry no smokers, two bit liars, no small time jokers... This train is bound for glory; this train."

Woody Guthrie

In the last verse of "This Land Is Your Land," Woody sings "As I went walking, I saw a sign there, And on the sign there, It said 'no trespassing.' But on the other side, it didn't say nothing! That side was made for you and me." Some teachers see themselves as the gate keeper to that property and not everyone is welcome, especially the under-served. Here is a story about a teacher who opened those gates for a fifth grader and gave her independence.

———————

"Some teachers changed my life but let me tell you, NONE of them were professors at U.C. Berkeley.

"The U.C. folks had absolutely no interest in undergrads. They were inaccessible, remote and clearly disinterested in everything but their 'publish or perish' objectives. If you wanted to learn you had to do it without any help from them. Fortunately I had a teacher who prepared me for that.

"I came from a poor family. My parents were immigrants. We were referred to as 'Greenhorns.' We were not given much attention by our teachers. One teacher told me to 'shoot for working in a factory because the children of greenhorns were good for that.'

"The most important teacher for me was a fifth grade teacher who told me that I was beautiful, brilliant and had a wonderful heart. She helped me see myself in a different light. She told me to believe in myself, to keep my eyes pointed forward, not down. She didn't just say it, but she showed it to me every day, in the way she challenged me and believed in me. As a kid from a very poor family living in the projects, her confidence in my abilities has meant all the difference. The other folks never offered any invitation, no pointing to ways to improve or see a positive future. She taught me how to succeed on my own.

"I am a lawyer now. Funny, though I did my undergrad and graduate work at U.C. Berkeley, I had to make it by myself. Now I work to help others find inspiration.

"My fifth grade teacher's faith in me has stayed with me. From those of us who know that a good teacher inspires..."

Renee S.

By Megan B., Age 7
British Columbia, Canada

My Dog Ate Them

Best excuses for why teachers
haven't handed back your tests

Most of us have had that teacher who just never seemed to be able to get your work back to you. Here are a few of the best excuses that people have experienced along the way, when the tests ultimately were never returned. To expose the humor in some of this is not to diminish the critical need for feedback, the loss of trust and respect, and the negative impact on learning when the expectation is not fulfilled.

"My wife has had my car all week because hers is in the shop. All my papers are in there so I couldn't get to them."

"I've met a new guy and I got asked out on a date and guess what – your tests lost out."

"We were away for the weekend and I wasn't able to get home to get them."

"I'm going to turn that test into a worksheet so you won't really need it. We'll do another test later."

I've decided not to count that test because it would have brought everyone's grades down."

"I Think that you have done such a
wonderful job, I've submitted them all
to be reviewed for publication. They
may not send them back to us."

"It didn't seem that you really cared –
I'll try to find them. If you don't care
why should I hand them back?"

"I can't find them, but don't worry – if
I can't find them you won't have to take
them over."

"I've decided to keep these test because
I want to be able to compare your work
now to your work on the final."

"I was correcting them while I was at the
beach over the weekend. This gust of
wind blew them all into the ocean."

Atri R., age 5
Massachusetts,USA

Trust And Connection

"Nothing is so hard for those who abound in riches as to conceive how others can be in want."

Jonathan Swift

This story makes a thoughtful transition from trust to connections. It takes a great deal of trust to accept someone's encouragement to do that which you don't believe you can. It also requires trust and a sense of connection to believe that they will follow-through on their promise to help you get there.

"My mother is Jewish and my father is a Palestinian. I grew up under the kind hand of tolerance that was an important part of my family. I have often wondered why the Jews and Arabs hate each other so much, when between my parents there is so much love. In our family, at times when others might not have so much, we would always spend part of our important days helping others. For example, on Thanksgiving, part of our day was spent at a homeless shelter helping to serve dinner to those who otherwise would have had none. This helped to teach me about helping others. I decided at some point that I wanted to be able to help reach people in the middle east, especially in Israel and Palestine.

"This of course would require that I learn Arabic. I don't know if you have ever heard it, let alone tried to speak it, but it seems almost impossible, and I knew it would be impossible for me. I genuinely believed that by learning Arabic I would be able to do more good, but learning Spanish or French would certainly have been easier. Also it wasn't offered at my school. I would have to take it at the local college. I didn't have enough confidence and decided to give up on the idea.

"Mr. Rashid was my history teacher. He is an Arab from Qatar. He knew of my interest in doing something to help people. He was also aware of my thoughts, through the many history discussions we had in class. When he heard that I was not going to study Arabic, he asked me to stop by his office.

"He spent a little time telling me how important he thought that my learning Arabic was, and he really encouraged me to do it. Then he said, or offered something that really made all the difference. First, he encouraged me to trust myself, to believe I could do it. Second, he promised he would meet with me during lunch and after school as much as I needed, to ensure that I was successful. It's important to point out that Arabic is his native language (although in Qatar there is a different dialect) but he also studied it at the university. In addition to trusting myself he was asking me to trust him.

"I did. I enrolled in the course. I worked very hard. You can't imagine how difficult the language is, even just making the sounds. He helped it make sense, helped me get the pronunciations. He even shared some of the idiomatic parts. He never let me down. I passed that course with an A and continued to study Arabic in college. Mr. Rashid stayed connected with me and spent time helping me raise grant money to go to Jordan to put together a program for Israelis and Palestinians to discuss how to see the humanity in each other. It took a lot of trust, but that trust changed me. Trust in each other is essential to be open to learning and to changing."

Sarah C.

Sri Lankan
refugee child

163

Did You Ever Have the Teacher

disConnected

Chapter Eight

"We cannot hold a torch to light another's path without brightening our own."

Ben Sweetland

Vernal Equinox

Not every learning experience is as it seems. We all have our memories when we were in school and some of the other students did a trick on the class or teacher. This story is about such a class who, as I found out, changed the laws of physics at the same time.

Most often, spring comes on March 21st. This was an odd year, this day was March 22nd and it was the first day of spring, the Vernal Equinox. In an attempt to discuss the underlying science I asked the question about the myth – Can an egg be made to stand on its tip on the vernal equinox?

We discussed where the sun was in relationship to Earth. We then asked did it really matter that the sun was traveling over the equator at that exact moment. Would its gravitational pull allow an egg to stand upright? Why couldn't it happen at other times? What would happen on the other equinox in the fall (the autumnal equinox)?

In anticipation of this discussion I had purchased a dozen eggs for each class. We went into the laboratory and each group tried to make an egg stand upright. A few eggs were broken fairly quickly, some groups achieved a second or two of success. But one group succeeded in getting an egg to stay upright and stationary, and it stayed like that for the remainder of the class and beyond.

As the story spread, each subsequent class was quite convinced that it was possible to stand an egg on its head on the vernal equinox. But at the end of the lab, I decided to discard the egg. To my surprise the upright egg provided quite a bit of resistance. In fact, I had to break the little drop of super glue that they had used to give this egg its unusual status, and connect it to the lab counter.

In order to demonstrate that there was no physical basis for this myth, I returned to the lab with the next class. Without the aid of super glue we attempted to reproduce the experiment. As you might guess we got the very same result as the first time, of course, with one group's results notably missing.

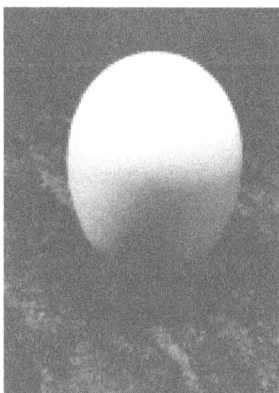

The Egg

Mrs. Rich

"Mathematics is the supreme judge; from its decisions there is no appeal."

Tobias Dantzig

———————

Ah, the dreaded trip to the board. This seems to be a common experience, teachers not listening or not being sensitive to kids who are panicked by the ordeal. The description is that their heads get filled with noise and they can't think. They are paralyzed. When there is no reprieve and it goes beyond panic, they begin to feel nauseated or dizzy. It becomes impossible to think.

They certainly cannot think about math … Think back to our "space invader" student (p. 95), it's all about "how can I get out of this situation." The experience is genuinely traumatic. Often teachers, either don't pick up on it, or they feel it's "important to push the student" to attempt to complete it. No matter how the ordeal ends, usually by being sent back to your seat, the student feels deep relief that it is over, and a sense of inadequacy. But they have escaped. Can you imagine what kind of effect this experience has on the ability to continue working on the material?

How much would they want to face their homework, pick up the book, and look at the looming source of fear and torture? These students describe having the sense of panic start up again even when they see the teacher outside of class. It's hard to imagine that a teacher would actually intend to do this and enjoy it. It's one of those things that if they knew what they were doing they would probably want to change the practice and its possible impact.

"Unfortunately I have a not-so-pleasant teacher experience. In the third grade we were learning multiplication tables in math. My teacher, Mrs. Rich, was a loud woman who liked to yell. She wore so much perfume that it made my head really hurt and she would never open the windows. Mrs. Rich picked on me every day to go up to the blackboard.

"She knew I was very shy and would embarrass easily. It seems though that she would never take that into consideration. It is hard to know whether she did this on purpose, and I have no idea what she got out of it or what she thought I got out of it. Every day when she would tell me to go to the board I would begin to panic. I was so nervous, and when I would get up to the blackboard, I felt nauseous. There was no way that I could answer the question. It was like there were two minds in me – the one trying to do the math and the one telling me I couldn't do it. I couldn't function. Sometimes I would get ill and run to the bathroom. Some days I didn't get sick but turned so white I would get sent home.

"There was no connection between me and her. I felt alienated and have hated math ever since. I've lacked confidence with anything sur-rounding it. Every math class after that was really difficult for me, but I was able to do much better in those classes where the teachers didn't make me have to be at the board. At the beginning of the school year I would try to tell teachers that I had this problem – sometimes it helped. I am now thirty years old and with the help of a math tutor I am preparing for a college entry exam. But that early trauma did have a long term impact."

Jeanette S.

Got Milk?

PEANUTS: © United Feature Syndicate, Inc.

The Grass is Always Greener...

"You may laugh at a man's roof, but don't laugh at the insides of his house."

Kenyan Proverb

For my sophomore year in high school, I spent a year at a British public school (an independent secondary school). It was called The Millfield School, in Street, Somerset Co. I was the only American there and was headed for trouble. I smoked (which I shouldn't have), had long hair and was interested in the local girls, all of which were not allowed. Well, these schools had a way of handling such infringements, *caning*. A "cane" was usually made of rattan, and at our school it was used to whip the transgressor across the buttocks. There was always a sense of dread that you would receive word to report for caning. You were guilty and had to prove yourself innocent. I got two strokes for refusing to cut my hair, and four when I was caught with cigarettes (not smoking, just having an empty pack). I was going to get six more for seeing a local girl (it was a coed school after all), when I decided to "terminate" my relationship with the institution. Many of the British Commonwealth countries, such as Kenya and Singapore, have continued the tradition of caning.

"We just moved here to the United States from Kenya. I am in the sixth grade. In Kenya, we have to go to primary school through to the eighth grade and at the end of the eighth grade we have to take a test to see whether we can go into secondary Andorra school. Most of my friends would not go on and didn't have to take that test.

"Some schools in Kenya are very good, and my family was able to send me to a school like that. We had good books. Sometimes they were better than the teachers, but we had good teachers too. Many other children had to go to a school called a Hamurabi school. At these schools the buildings were in very bad shape and there were no schoolbooks. Most of my friends at those schools didn't pass the fifth grade and didn't go on from school. Actually, I'm one of the few who passed the sixth grade.

"In the countryside the schools are very bad. My school was in the city. In my school there were many students from other countries. Some were from Kenyan families who lived outside Kenya. Many students were unable to go to school because they could not speak English. They could only speak in their local tribal language, even though English is the official language in Kenya.

"I am very happy to go to school in America. In America, when I come to class without my homework, they do not beat me."

Kigunda N.
Age 11

Jonathan K.,
Age 12
Tema, Ghana

Enthusiastic Teacher

"Yes! Did you ever have the teacher who managed to bore you to death even though you thought it was going to be a subject that you would really like? I have had subjects that I was interested in, outside of school, and even read about for fun. You're excited about taking the course, but then you get the killer teacher who just bores you to death, gives oppressive homework and hard tests. The subject stops being fun and starts to be a chore. But for me it was a teacher who did just the opposite.

"I'm talking about a teacher who can take a subject, that on the surface seems boring, yet is able to transmit to the student the life of the subject and their own genuine enthusiasm for it. Those are the good teachers, not just people who are competent in their field but who instill a love for the knowledge.

"I was looking for a class to fulfill my physical sciences requirement. The only one available to me, because of my schedule, was geology. My first reaction was – 'It's probably just about rocks.' I hoped that I would be able to keep awake in lecture. That's what I thought. Each chapter would be chock full of facts about rocks and I would simply be tortured having to memorize it all. Rocks! I foresaw a dismal time in this class.

"However, the teacher had a way of approaching the subject that was infectious. I couldn't help myself from becoming interested. She tied it into everything. It was kind of like being invited into seeing the world a whole new way. In between classes was like traveling on a new planet. She explained the material very clearly, and invited us to explore and ask questions that we found ourselves pondering. She would answer them enthusiastically and patiently.

"The way she was able to relate the material to our own lives made a big difference – earthquakes, the amount of damage they cause, improper adherence to building regulations, and then making connections. She was always having us handle various rocks. To us, they turned from being simple rocks into such things as calcite, gypsum, granite and even greensand (which is very beautiful). It was her showing us the love of geology that led me to attend a mineral convention, where I found an actual piece of meteorite to hang from my necklace.

"Sometimes I think that the ultimate accomplishment of a teacher is to make the subject come alive and generate student interest. We felt connected to this teacher and she made us feel connected to the subject matter and as a result more connected to the world. Oftentimes I think that boring teachers can't find the creativity and just settle with stuffing facts into student's heads without regard to whether there is any joy or not, and then testing for memory.

"It seems to me that one of the characteristics of a good teacher is that they can help us see and understand the world, and have it come alive."

Diana L.

Jakie Y., Age 7
Sabah, Malaysia

Younger Sister

"Big sisters are the crab grass in the lawn of life".

Charles M. Schulz

Over a series of years I had whole families come through my classroom. For each of seven years I had at least one member of the Putvain family. Some years I had two, one as a junior and one as a senior. They had very similar names: Trevor, Travis, Tamara and Traci. They all looked alike, and all were respectful and pleasant. But each was their own unique person. They understandably wanted to be recognized for who they were as individuals and wanted to feel known by their teacher.

The problem was that you would start to say one name and who knows which name would come out. You could see that slight look of disappointment. They always handled it well. I tried to develop strategies in order to avoid using a wrong name, like when you have twins in class. No doubt though, as in the story below, the results can be hurtful when done by a teacher who doesn't get it.

Another student I had was the very bright and delightful younger sister of one of the most difficult and troubled students in school. He "paved" the way for her. Her most difficult challenge was not being pigeon-holed as "cut from the same cloth" as her brother. She succeeded and eventually went through law school, but it was hard.

———————

You have probably heard many bad teacher stories similar to mine, but here it goes. It's not just one bad teacher, but many throughout the course of my education in a small Wisconsin town. And it's not that they were necessarily bad teachers in terms of information, but they did something that usually had a negative effect on me.

"I have an older sister who went through school just a year ahead of me. She's very ambitious and, quite frankly, an over-achiever. I don't harbor any ill feelings toward my sister, in fact I love her, but I do have very strong feelings toward all the teachers she had, who later wound up with me. I literally had a high school history teacher proclaim to my whole class how my sister had done very well on an assignment the year before. Then he asked me, again in front of the class, why I couldn't be more like her. Maybe it could be because we are two different people!

"I had one teacher though who went to great lengths to treat me as me. He always made the effort to connect with me (and I had felt so disconnected from my other teachers). He was a respite from what I faced every year.

"It is hard to communicate what these comparisons do to you. It takes all the wind out of your sails. It makes it so you don't even want to try because you will only be compared, and feel less about yourself. A teacher needs to treat each student as if they are their own person and not have to be like anyone who came before them. So, to help teachers be better educators, I suggest we keep sibling personality types separate. While the first one might set up expectations, good or bad, the second one has their own strengths that are different and need to be fostered. Prevent the second one from going through what I did. Stay conscious of it."

Carrie G.

The Twinkle of an Eye

"It is better to understand little than to misunderstand a lot."

Anatole France

Many students bring up the frustration with teachers who don't take into account that students have a life outside of school. First they get frustrated when they have a teacher who think that their's is the only course and they pile on the work. But also they feel misunderstood and under-cared-for when their personal lives interfere with school, and no one tries to understand. Often this conflict is not within their control. Perhaps they have siblings to care for, or absentee parents. I had a student who came late for a morning class. She had been to an early morning breakfast with her Mom, who was in prison, and security just took too long. Her first period teacher gave her a detention for being late. These outside circumstances take a toll. Even still, students want to feel that they are seen, believed in, and can still have hope. Here's Alondra's story

---

"My name is Alondra. I have never been a good student. I always wanted to be, but I found it hard. I couldn't concentrate and my family situation was really bad. Sometimes I couldn't get to school. Both my parents worked and it was my responsibility to get my little sister to the bus. I couldn't just leave her there so I would wait and often I was late for school.

"No one understood. There was other stuff. Sometimes my boyfriend wouldn't let me go. He told me that he didn't want me around other boys by myself. Sometimes he was physical. Anyway, most of my teachers just don't get it about the outside of school things.

"Anyway, most of my teachers didn't treat me very good about all this. They either treated me like I was no good or like I didn't even exist. When I did show up they never offered to include me in anything. Sometimes they just sent me to the office with make-up work to just sit there by myself and do it, even though I didn't know any of it. I knew I would never pass so why bother.

"I had one teacher though, Mr. Cowan, who made me feel completely different. When I showed up he was always happy to see me. He would involve me in something interesting. He would say, 'while I've got you here girl, let's do some learning.' He would try to find some way for me to be involved, along with the other students. No matter what, I always left his classroom feeling like maybe I could be a student, maybe I could be smarter. I know my outside situation was my own thing and my own problems are what kept me from getting anywhere in school, but what Mr. Cowan did, and the way he dealt with me, helped me keep a sense of myself alive.

"A few years after I dropped out (I was a senior and I didn't have enough credit to graduate). I got my GED and went to community college. Now I work as a secretary in a dentist's office and take courses at night to become a nurse. When I study, I think of the way Mr. Cowan would get me to work in class those days and I know that he helped me be able to be where I am now."

Alondra R.

Teach me a new word

"I am always ready to learn, but I do not always like being taught."

Sir Winston Churchill

No doubt the first couple of years of school are very important, and have life-long effects, both good and bad. I visited with a third grade class to explore with them what their experience with teachers had been so far. What sort of "teacher stories" did they have? While they haven't exactly had a lot of education, or teachers for that matter, to look back on, it seemed to me important to find out how they feel. What did these kids have to say?

Jakie Y., age 7
Sabah, Malasia

It was interesting just to be with them. I am a high school teacher and when I walked into the third grade class, It seems silly, but I was surprised to see a room full of very little people with bright eyes and anticipation. They had been told that there would be a guest in class that day to talk about their past teachers, and they were all very excited. They couldn't sit still nor did I want them to.

It brought flashes of my third grade and my teacher, Miss Byron. She was smart and attractive, and being in her class was a separate universe. She ran our world. Our whole day was spent with her in the classroom. I had Mrs. Corson for first grade and Miss Nadoe for the second, but Miss Byron was the first teacher I had with whom I felt like I was becoming a person. How she treated me was very formative. Third graders' needs, while perhaps more immediate and filled with an innocent eagerness, are no different than anyone else's.

As I mentioned with the last list, regardless of the group you ask, the issues, concerns, and the wishes all sound pretty familiar: don't be mean, don't humiliate me, be fair, and teach me something.

As for the questions I asked…

<u>What is the best thing that your teachers do?</u>

"Give us special treatment like giving us candy for no special reason,"

"Be patient with us and give us prizes for things that we do,"

"Do some easy and hard problems before making us take the homework home, and do some problems together,"

"Help me on my homework and talk to me when I am sad,"

"Give us lots of recess all the time.

What do teachers do that you wish they didn't?

> "Don't be too strict, mean and cranky, when they don't need to be,"

> "When they yell so loud that they can break our ear drums,"

> "Give us too little and easy homework,"

> "Embarrass you in front of your friends,"

> "Punish us and give us bad grades,"

> "I wish she wouldn't spit on us when she talks really loud,"

> "I wish they didn't make me sit on the bench at recess."

＞～～～＜

What is one thing your teacher did that made you unhappy?

> "She made me stand facing the wall for a long time."

What is one thing your teacher did that made you happy?

> "She taught me a new word every day."

Out of Juice

For some teachers there comes a time when they know it's not in them anymore to bring all the right stuff to the classroom . Here are a few stories about being "out of juice."

"Mr. Sinclair (History): The year I started drinking in my car. I would roll up the windows and sit in the east side of the parking lot. In the last space. There was coffee in the older thermos and scotch in the other, newer one. But... I would say that was a pretty good sign I definitely stopped caring. By the end of that year I knew I was burned out.

"Mr. Keroman (Mathematics): Early on. Second semester of my first year. It didn't take long.

"Mr. Pappas (Social Studies): Once I was on this strange acne medication. It was making me feel completely different from how I usually feel, which is fine. It came to a head one day when I was chaperoning a field trip to the Museum of Natural History. I was feeling strange and I got off the bus and for some reason started crying because I wasn't on the bus any longer. I didn't want to go into the museum, but I did. They were looking at me, the kids on my field trip. I felt shame. Whatever it was that's when I knew.

"Mr. Lewis (PE): I was standing there on the field and...I was standing out on the field in September and that's when the geese droppings aren't completely frozen yet, but they aren't so wet that they just leach into the field, but they're not solid yet either. It's not until late November when they actually freeze. So the droppings, which cover the field, were still slightly wet. Maybe four of these kids ever wear their soccer cleats, even after I asked them to. No one was wearing them that day. So these kids were sliding in this goose shit. And somehow one swallowed a piece, in a tackle or something, but it was all over his face. And I just, you know...I just hated that kid. I had to clean him up. (pause) Yeah, I guess that was the moment."

Ask Yourself

The last story was about what students would like from us. After having explored some issues touching on trust, boundaries, power, etc., maybe now is a good time to ask ourselves how we think we are doing as teachers, parents, employers, or as anyone in a position of inequality with learners. The point is that we have listened to learners' experiences so that we may be more reflective, and find ways to make the educational experience more substantial, fulfilling and positive. Let's ask ourselves "how are we doing." The following questions come from the stories. There are no correct answers, of course, because we each provide them for ourselves. But perhaps our answers might provide initial benchmarks for our continued self-evaluation as teachers.

○ Do you collaborate well with other colleagues?
○ Do you return students' work in a timely manner?
○ Do you give quality feedback that allows student to clearly understand how successful they have been with their work and what they need to do next?
○ Do you assign work to students they are not yet capable of completing?
○ Do you have favorites, or treat some students better than you treat others?
○ Do you use inappropriate discipline (e.g. using homework)?
○ Do you find yourself getting into arguments with students?
○ Do you "visit," make eye contact, communicate with all students, equally, over the course of a class? How do you evaluate this?
○ Do you have objective ways of assessing how well you're doing, other than just what you think, or hear from your students?
○ Do you differentiate between your popularity and your effectiveness as a teacher?
○ Are you clear about your boundaries in terms of closeness to students, perhaps even to particular students? What are they?
○ Do you have an objective way to know whether students are satisfied with what they are learning?
○ Do you engage in teaching/class management practices that may create boundaries that possibly compromise some students' access to you, and therefore their education?
○ Are you a gate-keeper, or a door opener, for student fulfillment?

"Music of My Heart"

"You'll never know, what you've done for me.
What your faith in me, has done for my soul.
You'll never know the gift you've given me.
I'll carry it with me.
Through the days ahead
I'll think of days before.
You made me hope for something better
And made me reach for something more.
You taught me to run
You taught me to fly..."

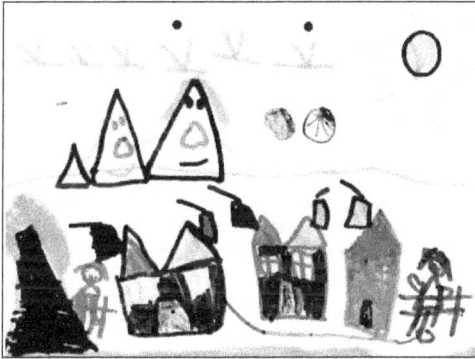

Hiu Ching Y., age 4
Hong Kong, China

The special teacher is the one who taught you "how to fly."

From www.nsync.com

Epilogue - My Teacher Story

"It is our responsibility as [teachers], knowing...the great progress that is the fruit of freedom of thought, to proclaim the value of this freedom, to teach how doubt is not to be feared but welcomed and discussed. To demand this freedom, is our duty to all coming generations."

Richard Feynman

I chose this quote as the introduction to my story because it highlights the great responsibility that falls to all of us as teachers to help doubt, and the unknown, become sources of excitement and not of fear. The challenge is to allow others to question and to have input, to find their way from the almost audible fog of ignorance, to the thrill of knowing, and to do it without intimidation or humiliation. If I've learned anything from this book, it is that intimidation and humiliation, in one form or another, get in the way of education.

Whether as a parent, a coworker, a health care giver, a teacher, or as an employer, we need to be compassionate, to give of ourselves, provide leadership, and to teach.

As you find yourself in a position to teach, whether conscious or not, it is likely that you will emulate the style of that teacher who meant the most to you. It is no different for me. I feel the presence of that teacher every time I stand in front of a group of students, give a presentation, or work one-on-one with someone. He was Mr. Beevers.

He was my ninth grade homeroom and "Social Studies" teacher. He grew up in a tough section of town. His father had died while he was young and his mother had an alcohol problem. There were lots of reasons for him not to have succeeded. Instead though he went to school for education and returned as a teacher, with a mission to help kids.

I suppose that I still see him through the eyes of a ninth grader although we were to become great friends as time went on. When someone was out of line he was very firm with them, but also used a stroke of humor. He was self-effacing and could laugh at himself as well. One day, Jimmy Gallagher, who had a penchant for being mean to others, got into an argument with Mr. Beevers, so he took Jimmy down to the gym. They donned boxing gloves and they had it out right there. Not in a way that anyone would be hurt, but it brought Jimmy down quite a few pegs. (Boundaries were a little different then).

We all knew his story because he shared it with us. He encouraged us not to drink, and invited us to participate with him in all sorts of school programs, especially athletics, (whether you were any good or not). He attended every game and every play, and made a point to know our parents and to understand our families; always being there to help in those kinds of struggles.

When I was in the 10th grade in a particularly bad stretch with my own family, Wally (his first name) and his wife Mary invited me to live with them, as my family worked out their problems. A few years later, while I was working as a photographer, he created an opportunity for me to come back to the school and teach a photography program to kids who were having trouble. What a great experience; it also helped me develop that "fire in the belly" to teach, and to emulate him as my mentor.

Times were different then and how he taught was different, but what he gave was universal. As a teacher I strive to give others what he gave me. He helped me be myself. He made me feel cared-for and guided, and he helped me develop a love for learning.

Noah H., age 6
Tennessee, USA

I am still in touch with him and recently shared the book. It made me realize how this process has been an experience of humility for me. My original intent was to create a vehicle for people to use as a mechanism for self-reflection, to find in these stories insights that could lead to improved teaching and a better educational experience for students. Instead, as each issue came up, I began to see the ways in which I needed to improve. It was kind of like being a first year medical or nursing student and thinking that you have each of the diseases that you study. Except in this case I was seeing within myself real things that I could change, or could do better.

What is not so much in the words from these stories, but is very clearly between them, is about the sacred trust that we have been given to provide our students an experience that adds to their quality of life, both now and in the future. The chapter titles are not frivolous. Trust, power, boundaries, empathy, etc., it is through these that students' educational experiences are either protected or harmed. It is in evaluating how well we are providing and protecting these, that we can help ensure our students are being treated with respect and fairness.

To violate, or fail to protect any one of those categories can lead to humiliation and loss of trust. And this failure, as we have read, is the sure-fired way to hinder the opportunity of a vulnerable person to learn.

Avoiding humiliation is a major goal. It is not just in education. The potential for humiliation lurks in the background of all human interactions. Being more sensitive to trust, to boundaries, and to student empowerment is the key to creating a safe, all inclusive learning environment. This does not mean that there are not abusive and over-empowered students, but it does imply that creating the right environment starts with

Gabby B., age 6
Massachusetts, USA

Gabby's picture of me

ourselves in the process of being better teachers and better people. Thank you for the opportunity to have shared this journey of self-reflection.

Reference to the Quotes

Alcott, Louisa May – (November 29, 1832 - March 6, 1888) Born in Germantown, PA, author of "Little Women" and "Little Men." p 16

Alber, Rebecca – Consulting online editor of Edutopia.com and teacher of online education at Stanford. p 150

Angelou, Maya – (April 4, 1928-) born in St. Louis, Missouri, as Marguerite Ann Johnson, is an American autobiographer and poet. p 62

Anthony, Susan Brownell – (February 15, 1820 – March 13, 1906) was a prominent American civil rights leader in the 19th century movement for women's suffrage in the United States. p 134

Bacon, Roger – (1214 - 1294) Born in Ilchester, Somerset, Eng., he was known as "Doctor Mirabilis" (astounding teacher), an English philosopher, scientist, and Franciscan monk. p 82

Barzun, Jack – Born in 1907, he is an author and active voice in Literature, education, and cultural history. p 108

Blackwell, Lawana – Born in 1952, she is an author; the quote is from "The Dowry of Miss Lydia Clark," 1999. p154

Bloch, Robert Albert (April 5, 1917 – September 23, 1994) was a prolific American writer, primarily of crime, horror and science fiction. p 121

Brautigan, Richard Gary – (November 30, 1935 - September 14, 1984) Born in Tacoma, Washington. He was a 20th century American novelist, poet, and short story writer. p 89

Browne, Merry – Born 1921, she is an author. p 77

Buddha – (Siddhartha Gautama) (about 623 BCE to 543 BCE) Born in Lumbini, India, he was the historical founder of Buddhism. p 143

Burney, Robert – Born in 1948, he is an author, teacher and codepedency therapist, author of "The Dance of Wounded Souls." p 72

Carruthers, Thomas – Biography unavailable, p 63

Churchill, Winston R. – (November 39, 1874 - January 24, 1965) Born in Oxfordshire, England, he was a soldier, politician and British Prime minister. p 178

Dantzig, Tobias – (February 19, 1884 – August 9, 1956) Born in Latvia, he was a mathematician, who studied under Poincare and others. p 167

Demmings, W. Edward – (October 14, 1900 – December 20, 1993) Born in Sioux City, Iowa, he became an engineering professor at MIT and father of the TQM (Total Qualitiy Management) movement, p 60

Disney, Walt – (December 5, 1901 - December 15, 1966). Born in Chicago, IL., he was an animator, movie maker, and creator of the Disney theme parks. p 58

Donatus, Aelius – Lived 4th century AD, he was an ancient Roman grammarian, author of several school grammer books which were used for almost a thousand years. p 86

Durant, Will – (November 5, 1885 - November 7, 1981). Born in North Adams, MA, he was an American writer and philosopher who worked for social justice. p 33

Dylan, Bob – Born Robert Allen Zimmerman - (May 24, 1941), in Deluth, MN, he is an American singer/songwriter, musician and poet. p 64

Edwards, Tyron – (Aug 7, 1809 - January 4, 1894) Born in Hartford, Connecticut, He was an American theologian and Educator, best known for compiling the "New Dictionary of Thoughts." p 52

Einstein, Albert – (March 14, 1879 - April 18, 1955) Born in Württemberg, Germany, he was a preemminent American physist and philosopher. p 36, 97, 100, 140

Eliot, Thomas Stearns, OM (September 26, 1888 – January 4, 1965) was an American born poet, playwright, and literary critic, perhaps the most important English language poet of the 20th century. p 144

Emerson, Ralph Waldo – (May 25, 1803 - April 27, 1882), Born in Boston, Massachusetts, he was an American author, philosopher and thinker. p About the Book, and p 130

Feynman, Richard (May 11, 1918 – February 15, 1988) Born in Far Rockaway, Queens, New York. He was a world reknown physicist in quantum mechanics and was involved in the development of the atomic bomb. p 184

France, Anitole – (Jacques Anatole François Thibault) (1844-1924) - Born in Paris, he was a French poet, journalist, and novelist. p 176

Frost, Robert Lee – (March 26, 1874 – January 29, 1963) an American poet. Born in San Francisco, moved to Lawrence, MA and then to Vermont. His epitaph quotes a line from one of his poems: "I had a lover's quarrel with the world." p 15 & p 95

Gauguin, Paul (June 7, 1848 – May 8, 1903) Born in Paris, he was a post-impressionistic painter. p 84

Gibran, Khalil (January 6, 1883 – April 10, 1931) Born in Bsharri, Lebanon, he was a Lebanese American artist, poet, and writer. p 31

Goethe, Johann Wolfgang von – (August 28, 1749 – March 22, 1832) Born in Frankfurt, Germany, he was a German writer, scientist, mathematician, philosophist, and theologian. p 28

Goldstein, Neil (1954 -) Quoted while a student at Antioch College. Currently a Principle Scientist at Spectral Sciences Incorporated. p 104

Guthrie, Woodrow Wilson (July 14, 1912 – October 3, 1967) Born in Okemah, OK, an American singer-songwriter and folk musician and social advocate. p 158

Harris, Thomas A. (April 11, 1940 –) An American author and screenwriter, whose most notable work is "The Silence of the Lambs." p 48

Johannot, Louis – Director of the Institut Le Rosey, Rolle, Switzerland. p 136

Jung, Carl Gustav (July 26, 1875 – June 6, 1961) Born in Kesswil, Switzerland was a psychiatrist, an influential thinker and the founder of analytical psychology. p 132

Kozol, Jonathan (September 5, 1936 –) Born in Boston, Massachusetts, a non-fiction writer, educator, and activist. p 126

Krishnamurti, Jiddu (May 12, 1895 – February 17, 1986) Born in Madanapalle, India, was a renowned writer and speaker on philosophical and spiritual subjects. p 119

Leibniz, Gottfried Wilhelm – (July 1, 1646 – November 14, 1716) Born in Leipzig, Germany, a German philosopher, and mathematician. p 148

Lewis, Clive Staples – (November 29, 1898 – November 22, 1963) Born in Belfast, Ireland. Known to his friends and family as Jack, he was a British novelist, academic, medievalist, literary critic, essayist, lay theologian and Christian apologist. p 20

Levertov, Denise – (October 24, 1923 – December 20, 1997) Born in Ilford, Essex, England, was a British-born American poet. p introduction

Locke, John – (August 29, 1632 – 28 October 28, 1704) Born in Wrington, Somerset, he was an English philosopher and physician regarded as one of the most influential of Enlightenment thinkers. p 44

Lombardi, Vincent Thomas – (June 11, 1913 – September 3, 1970) Born in Brooklyn, NY, he was an American football coach. p 42

Lutz, William – (December 12, 1940 –) Born in Racine, Wisconsin, he is an American linguist who specialized in the use of plain language and the avoidance of doublespeak (deceptive language). p 102

Maugham, William Somerset – (January 25, 1874 – December 16, 1965) Born in Paris (but in the British embassy so as to avoid French citizenship) was an English playwright, novelist and short story writer. p 35

McCullers, Lulla Carson – (February 19, 1917 – September 29, 1967) Born in Columbus, Georgia, she was an American writer. p 92

Nin, Anais – (February 21, 1903 – January 14, 1977) Born (Angela Anaïs Juana Antolina Rosa Edelmira Nin y Culmell) in Neuilly, France, she was a French author, famous for her journals and erotica. – opening quote & pg 123

Ovid – (Publius Ovidus Naso) (March 20, 43 BCE – ca. 18 CE. Born in Sulmo, Roman Republic, he was a Roman poet. p 66

Sargent, John Singer – (January 12, 1856 – April 14, 1925) Although he had American parents, he was born in Florence, Italy. He was an American painter, especially as a protrait painter. p 25

Shakespeare, William – (ca. 1564 – April 23, 1616) Born in Stratford-upon-Avon, England, was an English poet and playwrite. p 106

Shulz, Charles M. – (November 26, 1922 – February 12, 2000) Born in Minneapolis, MN, he was a cartoonist and the creator of the Peanuts series. p 174

Sweetland Ben – Widely known for his syndicated column "The Marriage Clinic" and his many books, including I Will, and I Can, and Get Rich While You Sleep. p 165

Swift, Jonathan – (November 30, 1667 – October 19, 1745) Born in Dublin, an Anglo-Irishman who became a satirist, essayist, political pamphleteer, poet, & priest. p 162

Talbert, Robert – is a mathematician and educator, and currently an Associate Professor of Mathematics and Computing Science at Franklin College in Franklin, Indiana. p 22

Thoreau, Henry David – (July 12, 1817 – May 6, 1862) born in Concord, MA, he was an American author, poet, naturalist, tax resister, development critic, surveyor, historian, philosopher, and leading transcendentalist. p 50

Tomlin, Mary Jean "Lily" (September 1, 1939 –) Born in Detroit, Michigan, she is an American actress, comedian, writer and producer. p 116

Twain, Mark – Actually Samuel Langhorne Clemens (November 30, 1835 – April 21, 1910). Born in Florida, Missouri, he was an American author and humorist. p 56

Warren, Eric – A client of the American Institute for Stuttering, who is also blind. p 68

Winchell, Walter – (April 7, 1897 – February 20, 1972) Born in New York, NY, he was an American newspaper and radio commentator. p 24

Yehoshua, Abraham B. – (December 19, 1936 –) is an Israeli novelist, essayist, playwright, and ardent peace activist. His pen name is A. B. Yehoshua. p 80

Additional Resources from Navigating Learning

Special pricing for Education Programs, Book Clubs, and other group sales, contact:
Groupsales@Navigatinglearning.com
Navigatinglearning.com/Groupsales.

Schools, Clubs & Groups

Book Store Sales, contact:
Bookstores@Navigatinglearning.com
Navigatinglearning.com/Bookstores.

Book Store Sales

If you would like to order an extra copy of this book
order@Navigatinglearning.com
Navigatinglearning.com/order.

Extra Copies

Did You Ever Have the Teacher…makes a wonderful gift to anyone who cares about how we influence and care for those of us we teach. We will gift wrap it, include a card and send it as a gift from you. email: giftsales@Navigatinglearning.com or go to: Navigatinglearning.com/giftsales.

Gift Copies

Navigating Learning

phone 413-629-5690
toll-free 888-854-6261
NavigatingLearning.com
Info@navigatingLearning.com

Educational Inservice and Corporate Workshops available - see other side

Additional Resources from Navigating Learning

Educational Inservice

Navigating Learning makes half-day or after school professional development activities available to schools. Sharing our teacher stories and how our teachers might have influenced us is a wonderful way to explore our own teaching, and our impact on students. It is both humorous and serious, in a sharing environment.
If interested, contact
Inservice@Navigatinglearning.com

Corporate Workshops

Navigating Learning makes half-day corporate workshops available in-house, and for conferences and retreats. Using our teacher stories is an insightful and fun way to explore how we treat our fellow workers, our employees, and our employers. We are influenced by how we have been treated. Our shared stories can help us find ways to improve our interpersonal lives at work.
If interested, contact
Workshops@Navigatinglearning.com

Navigating Learning Educational Publishing is committed to helping put quality educational products in the hands of those who need them. If you have an educationally relevant manuscript, game, or other product and would like to explore working with us, please use the information below.

Navigating Learning
phone 413-629-5690
toll-free 888-854-6261
NavigatingLearning.com
Info@navigatingLearning.com

Additional book sales information available on the reverse side

www.ingramcontent.com/pod-product-compliance
Lightning Source LLC
Chambersburg PA
CBHW030012290326
41934CB00005B/307